The Moral Disciple

The Moral

Disciple

An Introduction to Christian Ethics

KENT A. VAN TIL

WILLIAM B. EERDMANS PUBLISHING COMPANY
Grand Rapids, Michigan / Cambridge, U.K.

Published 2012 by

WM. B. EERDMANS PUBLISHING CO.

2140 Oak Industrial Drive N.E., Grand Rapids, Michigan 49505 /

P.O. Box 163, Cambridge CB3 9PU U.K.

Printed in the United States of America

16 15 14 13 12   7 6 5 4 3 2 1

Library of Congress Cataloging-in-Publication Data

Van Til, Kent A.

The moral disciple: an introduction to Christian ethics /

Kent A. Van Til.

     p.   cm.

ISBN 978-0-8028-6675-2 (pbk.: alk. paper)

1. Christian ethics.   I. Title.

BJ1251.V36   2012

241 — dc23

                              2012006676

www.eerdmans.com

For four generations of women who practice
Christian morality at least as well
as I teach Christian ethics

Minnie Recker Zwier
Linda Zwier Van Til
Kathleen Boelkins Van Til
Emily, Marie, and Anna Van Til

Contents

Foreword

I wish I had been able to assign this fine book by Kent Van Til to my ethics classes when I first started teaching college students over four decades ago.

The move from studying ethics as a philosophy graduate student to teaching the subject to large classes of undergraduates was for me a frustrating experience. I was prepared to lecture on the likes of Jeremy Bentham, John Stuart Mill, Immanuel Kant—all of them seen through the grid of the "meta-ethical" explorations that preoccupied the Oxford and Ivy League moral philosophers of the day. My students, however, came to class with many urgent moral dilemmas. Many of them were struggling with the unrest over the Vietnam War and the emerging environmental issues, to say nothing of questions of personal sexuality and vocational choices. And superimposed on all of that was the fact that I was teaching in a Christian liberal arts setting, where I was expected to relate all of my subject matter to biblical teachings in the context of a commitment to historic Christian orthodoxy.

I struggled in those days to put all of this together in a coherent Introduction to Ethics "package." I think I succeeded—at least to some small degree. But it wasn't easy. And not the least of my challenges was trying to find readings that actually displayed the kind of integration—of the philosophical, the practical, and the biblical-theological—that I was trying to manage. I was working without any robust models of what success would look like.

If I had such a model available to me at the time, I'm convinced that it would look almost exactly like the discussion in this book. And to say "almost exactly" is not to detract from the praise I am offering here. This book not only puts together the pieces that I was trying to work with in the early 1970s, but it also adds some new things. More recent discussions in ethics have paid sustained attention to "the virtues," to character formation, and this subject gets solid treatment in these pages. In my more youthful efforts, I did quite a bit with faith—meaning Christian faith—versus "secular" ethics. Van Til not only takes that discussion to a new level, with careful attention to the rich resources available to the Christian community, but he also rightly pays attention to the plurality of faiths, with, for example, frequent references to Muslim thought and practice. And in all of that, he offers practical examples, including some helpful case studies, that highlight key concerns in this period of what he accurately identifies as "late modernity."

I cannot leave off, however, without confessing a bit of envy relating to my sense that Kent has written a better book on this subject than I could have produced. I feel compelled to make that confession in order to be clear about the fact that reading this book has made me more sensitive to the need for more moral honesty in my own soul!

RICHARD J. MOUW

PART ONE

Introducing Christian Ethics

CHAPTER ONE

What Is Ethics?

FEW PEOPLE WISH to be seen as judgmental, or as imposing their sense of morality onto someone else. And in many modern countries it is considered more than bad manners to suggest that morality should be based on religious beliefs. Those who do base morality on religious beliefs may be seen as intolerant.

Nevertheless, humans are naturally moral creatures. That is to say, we do right and wrong, or good and evil, and we know that we do. We perform moral acts because we were raised in communities that taught us what morality is, and some of these communities are specifically religious. We have developed habits, good and bad. We act in certain ways because we have accepted someone or something as a moral standard for our actions. We do things we believe will produce good for ourselves and others. So to be human is to be moral. In fact, as far as we can see, we may be the only moral creatures in the cosmos! That is quite a responsibility.

"Who gives you the right to judge . . . ?"
"Live and let live."
"You can't legislate morality."
"Whatever. . . ."

Is the study of ethics simply a nonstarter? Do you believe that it's possible to make moral judgments at all?

A Definition of Ethics

You have probably used the terms *ethical, moral,* and *immoral* on many occasions. For example: "He is the most immoral person I have ever met," or "She holds herself to a pretty high standard of ethics." But what do these terms address? The answer is that they have to do with issues of right and wrong, virtue and vice, and good and evil. We are asking moral questions when we say, What is the right thing to do here? Who is responsible? Is good or bad going to result from it? Am I acting with integrity if I do this?

Notice that these questions are not about subjects like beauty, or strength, or profit. For instance, you may judge that your light blue shirt goes better with your jeans than your brown shirt. But while it might be true that the blue shirt is a better match than the brown, that truth is not a moral truth or a moral judgment. It is a truth and judgment about style and/or beauty. In the same category are questions such as whether one truck is better for the job than another, or whether one cleanser is more effective on your carpet than another. These are evaluative questions, but they evaluate mechanical, aesthetic, and chemical values, not moral ones.

What, then, is *ethics?* Am I making a grammatical error by using a singular verb ("is") with a plural subject ("ethics")? No, the term *ethics* is not plural. It is derived from the Greek term *ethos*, which means "character." At its linguistic root, then, ethics is the evaluation of character.

Terms

Mores: shared manners, habits, and customs
Ethos: the character of a person or group
Norm: whatever serves as a model or pattern, a type or a standard

Morality and ethics are very similar; in fact, in common usage the terms are often interchanged. *Morals* are the actual manners, habits, and customs of humans that relate to right and wrong, good and evil. *Ethics* is more accurately understood as a systematic evaluation of the goodness or evil, the rightness or wrongness of human behavior. As a botanist studies plant life and a psychologist studies the human psyche, so an ethicist studies moral life. All normal adults are moral beings, because we all have norms and habits for behaviors that can be evaluated in terms of good or evil, right or wrong. Those who reflect on these motivations, actions, and outcomes are studying ethics.

Is ethics, then, a description of human actions? No. Sociologists and anthropologists are in the business of describing and explaining social mores, but their work typically does not attempt to evaluate the rightness or wrongness of them. The study of ethics evaluates actions, motives, and consequences according to standards of right and wrong. Ethics does not just describe or explain — it judges. Ethics also does not address many human actions that are *amoral*. For example, tossing a pencil up in the air and then catching it is not a moral action. You did indeed perform an action, but it had no moral quality to it. Your action did obey some laws — the law of gravity and other physical laws — but it had nothing to do with morality. If an action is a moral action, it must have qualities like good and bad or right and wrong to it.

Let me give you another example. Say that my teenage daughter has promised me that she will be home by 11:30 P.M. on nights when she goes out. However, on one particular night, there's a storm that blows a tree branch down onto the road she usually takes home. So she's delayed until 12:30 A.M. because she has to take a wide detour. If this is the case, her coming home late isn't wrong. It's the result of a natural incident. Cars don't leap over large trees, and she isn't responsible for the storm, so her late return is an *amoral* event. On the other hand, if she decides that she's having so much fun with her friends that she wants to stay until the party ends around 1:00 A.M., she is acting immorally. In this case, there is no natural obstruction blocking her return; she is responsible for the decision that causes her to be late and thus break her promise. What she does in the second instance is *immoral*. She has performed an action that is not in accord with the established moral standard that she and I agreed on. She has acted against the *mores* of our household, one of which is to keep your promises.

There are some things that are immoral no matter whose house you're in. These *moral norms* apply quite widely. Determining what these are and why they are relevant is one important aspect of ethics. For example, I can think of no circumstances in which it would be right to kill a thriving child: to do so would be *immoral,* no matter where it occurred or who did it.

Here's a summary for now: ethics is a systematic evaluation of moral issues, and a moral issue must include a person who is accountable. The term *moral* has two counterparts: *amoral* and *immoral. Amoral* describes an action that has no moral quality to it; *immoral* means

Amoral · · · · · · · · · Moral · · · · · · · · · · Immoral
Has no moral aspects   Fits moral norms
Has moral aspects   Opposes moral norms

that an action has a moral quality to it — that is, the quality of being opposed to a moral standard.

Are human *actions*, then, the only things that ethics studies? No, ethics also studies the motives, virtues, and vices that generate the actions — or the inaction. For example, perhaps you have the virtue of patience. This gives you the capacity to react to events in a deliberate and careful way. If, however, you have the vice of being hot-tempered or rash, you might react too quickly and harm yourself or others. The *ethos* of a person refers to her character, and character is an important aspect of ethics.

Ethics is not only about decisions; it is also about our moral formation over time. We can shrink or grow in virtue. We can become more or less law-abiding. We can generate more or less good. Therefore, ethics is both a snapshot of the morality of particular decisions on given occasions and a lifelong movie of the kind of moral persons we are becoming.

Christian Faith and Ethics

Earlier in the church's history, ethics was not a distinct field of study, though it was always present. In fact, being a Christian disciple automatically raised ethical questions. Christians have always asked, How shall we follow Christ? What does it mean to be disciplined in Christian virtue? What is the right or the good that God would have me do? These are both old and new ethical questions, and they have both old and new answers. The fact that they are new is due to the differences of our culture and our individual context. Yet they are old because both Old Testament and New Testament believers have asked and answered similar questions.

The Bible uses many metaphors and similes that encourage us to develop a Christian morality. It tells us to "put on Christ," "follow Christ," "be transformed into the likeness of Christ," "love one another," and so on. Narrative passages in Scripture often call us to share in the life of God's people, both ancient and modern. The Bible calls us to lives of holiness and justice and love and virtue. This book is a systematic study of these subjects. It is my hope that you, by interacting with this text, will become more clear about and conscious of your moral life.

This is specifically a study of *Christian* ethics. If I refer to "red ball," you quickly have a picture of the object I'm talking about: it is more than likely round and probably bounces, and it has the characteristic of redness. When I say "Christian ethics," I'm using the name of a religion as an adjective for a field of study. Biology and history are also fields of study, so when I say "Christian ethics" I am saying something about the kind of ethics that I am about to do, such as *micro*-biology or *ancient* history. The adjective "Christian" will direct this study of ethics at every point. I will look at the whole subject of ethics from the point of view of a Christian. I will be wearing "Christian glasses," you might say.

Morality and Salvation

Since there is a difference between morality and salvation, this book will not address the process, for example, of becoming filled with the Holy Spirit; nor is it about the Rule of Saint Benedict. This book also does not assume that Christians don't need to study ethics since they are saved. True, Christians are by nature perfected. Unfortunately, it is not true that being a Christian means that you are exceptionally moral; nor does it mean, inversely, that being a non-Christian assumes that you are immoral. This is because morality and salvation are two different things. Being a Christian is an absolute category. It addresses one's standing before God: either you are reborn in Christ or you are not. Morality, however, is a different category. Morality focuses on human actions and virtues that can be evaluated in terms of right and wrong or good and evil apart from one's standing before God. All humans do things that are right and wrong, or good and evil, regardless of whether they are Christian.

For example, let us imagine that one person steals an ice-cream cone from a child; let's imagine that another person actually steals the child. It may be that the person who steals the ice-cream cone is a non-Christian and that the person who kidnaps the child is a Christian. All of the following could yet be true: both the Christian and the non-Christian did wrong; the Christian did something that was far more evil than what the non-Christian did; and yet the Christian will inherit eternal life, but the non-Christian will not.

Martin Luther used the phrase "at the same time justified and a sinner" to describe Christians. This dilemma is the source of our moral problem: we are both good and evil, we do right and wrong, and we are virtuous and vicious. It means that, as Christians, we can do moral evil, and a non-Christian can do moral good. It does not mean that someone is a Christian because he does good, or not a Christian because he does evil. The fact that Christians do evil has long puzzled theologians, as Luther's statement shows. The fact that we are simultaneously saved and sinners is due to the distinction between the categories of salvation and morality. Being able to do moral good does not require Christian faith, and doing evil does not presume the absence of faith. Salvation is granted on the basis of God's gift, which is received in faith. As Saint Paul insisted, even our good works add up to nothing before God and thus cannot save us (see Rom. 3:9–4:25). But people do good and evil regardless of their standing in Christ. Therefore, not all deeds done by Christians are necessarily good, nor are all those performed by non-Christians necessarily bad. Furthermore, good works performed by Christians do not save them, nor do bad deeds damn them.

Moral "Weight"

Although many actions do in fact have moral aspects, most have very little moral *weight*. That is, not all moral actions are equally important. If my daughter arrives home late, this is a little moral blip that has consequences for her and me, but those consequences won't extend beyond our house. On the other hand, some moral choices have profound consequences for thousands or even millions of people, as well as animals and plants. Mao Zedong, for example, decided to use his Red Guards to revolutionize China in 1966. This entailed the forced migration of hundreds of thousands of Chinese from their professional work in Chinese cities to hard labor in rural communes. Thousands died; families were torn apart; careers, homes, and natural settings were destroyed. That moral action had enormous evil consequences.

It may be that we do not know if our deeds will have much moral import. For example, if I am a technician at work in a science lab mixing chemicals for an experiment that I did not design, it may seem that there is very little moral content to my action. But if I know that the experiment is to produce a life-saving vaccine for those with AIDS, my actions take on moral significance. This is because they have *consequences* whose effects can be good or evil. On the other hand, if I know that the experiment I am performing has the intended consequence of setting off an explosion that will kill thousands of people, it could be immoral for me to perform that experiment.

Right and Wrong, Good and Evil

Ethics studies the moral capacities people have and the choices they make. There are three basic aspects to this that I derive from classical ethics: (1) the *virtue* of the moral agent; (2) a *standard* of right and wrong based on duty/norm; and (3) the *consequences* of good or evil. It may be obvious that the first category of personal virtue is not equal to the second or third categories of standards and consequences. It is not as obvious, however, that a standard and a consequence are as dissimilar. Right or wrong is the standard for the deed itself, whereas the category for consequences of our deeds is good or evil. They are not the same in a couple of ways. First, right and wrong is an absolute category, whereas good and evil is a relative one. Something can't be a little right, but more wrong. For example, three plus three is not relatively seven; it is exactly and only six. Any answer but six is wrong. So, too, in ethics: rights cannot be a little bit right or a little bit wrong. They must be one or the other. I recognize that there may be great dispute over whether a particular action is right or wrong, but that is not to say that something can be simultaneously right and wrong. Rather, it is a question of which standard of right and wrong is used, and whose perceptions are in play.

On the other hand, the category of good and evil is quite relative, and our language even suggests this. By paying attention to our use of language, we can see that there is a wide range in the scale of good and evil. If I snitch a little ice cream from a child's cone, I have done something wrong. But the wrong is not nearly so evil as if I were to kidnap that child. While both are wrongs, one is far more evil than the other. In addition, right/wrong and good/bad are two *kinds* of categories. They measure different things. Right and wrong measure how an act stands up against a standard or norm. Good and evil measure the effects that an action has. Putting this into the format that I set up earlier, the categories of right and wrong relate to norms, whereas good and evil relate to consequences.

Levels of Ethics

The study of ethics occurs at different levels. For example, take the case of a manager who has to make a tough decision about a valuable employee. Say that this employee has been caught using a corporate computer to search for sex partners online. This is quite a specific issue: a particular person and action are involved. The setting and circumstances are clear. Ethics with this degree of specificity is sometimes called *applied ethics*. It addresses a specific context in which a specific set of norms apply. Professional ethics are applied to a great diversity of subjects: bioethics, medical ethics, business ethics, technology ethics, legal ethics, and so forth.

At another level, you might address this moral issue as it relates to the use of property. You may agree that there are norms for the use of property that derive from Christian faith or civil law. You may recognize that there is corporate, private, and public property. But you might raise questions about where the rights of individuals intersect with those of corporations or government. You may debate how the right to property of individuals or corporations applies to cases such as the one mentioned above. At this level you are engaged in *normative ethics.*

At a higher level still, you may ask about the relationships between property and humans. What is a person? Why should we have particular relationships to property? Are corporations persons? Are the norms derived from communism or capitalism best for using property? Are there universal standards that all people ought to adhere to? What is it that justifies using these norms? At this quite abstract level, the issues are those of *meta-ethics.*

All three levels of ethical reflection might come into play in this case. Typically, the higher levels of ethical reflection are assumed rather than examined. But these higher levels of ethi-
cal reflection are indeed present. The order — from the broadest questions down to the most specific questions — is shown in the illustration. This book will move between meta-ethics and normative ethics. (There are many other books on different profes-sional ethics.)

Levels of Ethics

Meta-ethics
↑
Normative ethics
↑
Applied ethics

Foundational Moral Experiences

In the vast majority of cases, we don't engage in deep ethical reflection when considering moral issues. Our moral sense is enough. Whether we ought to steal sound equipment from our neighbor's house doesn't require a soul-searching investigation. It's wrong, and we know it. Nor are we very puzzled about whether we should run down the angry old man crossing the street. It, too, is clearly wrong.

But some questions do trouble us, and they merit careful consid-eration. What should we do about our friend who is pregnant and considering an abortion? Can't we look at a little pornography now and then? Do we really have to declare all of our income for tax purposes?

There is often a gut response when we face issues such as these. Our emotions make us uncomfortable, and we feel un-ease. These feelings become the starting point for ethical reflection. What do we sense? Why do we feel uncomfortable? Humans feel, and we sense. We are proud or ashamed, puzzled or certain, delighted or downcast. It is this initial sense of disquiet that often starts the process of ethical discernment.

Our feelings about morality give us an interesting starting point for our study. Feelings can deceive, or they can enlighten. Perhaps you were raised to show very little emotion. The first step in your ethical journey may then be to open yourself up to the pains of evil and the joys of good. The enemy of good morality is not really bad morality; we can always argue from bad to good. The real enemy of good morality is apathy and indifference. "Who cares?" and "So what?" are far greater challenges to ethics than is a bad moral choice.

Christian ethicist Daniel Maguire has defined ethics as "the art-science which seeks to bring sensitivity and method to the search for moral values" (Maguire, p. 6). In this definition, Maguire recognizes that we are always searching for moral values, and that our search is not only science, but art. We cannot turn to a computer or perform a complex calculation and come up with a moral judgment. We need to be sensitive to our moral scenery. That is, we need to notice the morality and immorality around us, and occasionally we must allow our pulses to rise. But sensation alone is not enough, either; we need method. I hope that in this book I can help you become both more sensitive and more methodical about your ethical practice.

Experiment

Take your resting pulse. Now read the following story.

66

Julie, a single woman in her early thirties, lives with her father, who suffers from dementia. She is his care-giver, but she likes to go out with friends. When she does, he is home alone, sometimes for fourteen hours at a time. During that time he wets and dirties himself. He is hungry but can't feed himself. He cries out for his wife, who has died years earlier. He is angry and screams at the neighborhood children. Meanwhile, Julie is at a party.

Wait ten seconds. Take your pulse again. Is it elevated?

60

Ethics and Philosophy

Ethics is one of the main branches of philosophical inquiry. Philosophers have long asked, "What is the good life?" and "What is justice?" Their answers come from a few potential sources: their own experience, their reason, and the history of previous answers to these questions. Christian theological ethics (there are also, e.g., Jewish and Muslim theological ethics) also uses experience, reason, and history, but assumes that divine revelation is a source for ethical knowledge. As a rule, what makes theological ethics different from philosophical ethics is the explicit role that theological ethics assigns to revelation and doctrine. The Christian ethicist makes explicit use of biblical and theological sources for her work; the philosophical ethicist would not do so. This is not to say that philosophical and theological ethics need be opposed to one another. A Christian ethicist who is a philosopher might well base his ethics on assumptions about Christian anthropology and norms, but argue in such a way that non-Christian readers would find his arguments reasonable without a direct appeal to revelation.

Within philosophical ethics, three great traditions (mentioned previously) have emerged: virtue ethics, duty ethics, and consequence ethics. Virtue ethics focuses on the *character* of the actor; duty ethics focuses on the *norms* for behavior; and consequence (or utilitarian) ethics focuses on the *outcomes*. My reason for using this system is straightforward. Looking at ethics in this way uses a structure that thinkers in the Western world have developed over a period of centuries. Constant reflection on ethics by both Christians and non-Christians has developed around these three themes.

Though the variations on these themes have been innumerable, the basic themes themselves are constantly being sounded, as though these thinkers have built an ethical house. They have shown that every house needs a floor and walls and a roof. So anyone today who studies ethics must use the same general structure as those who have built such houses in the past. As a Christian of late modernity, however, I will view these subjects differently from the way many non-Christian philosophers did. I think you will see that, at every step along the way, the Christian faith directs this study, and each section will be distinctly Christian.

Three Great Traditions

The great philosophical works of the Greeks, such as Plato's *Republic* and Aristotle's *Nichomachean Ethics*, have shaped our world and continue to shape the world of ethical studies. The three great traditions of ethics — virtue, duty, and consequence — have their intellectual origins in ancient Greece, and scholars today continue to use their Greek-derived names: *Areteology* (virtue), *De-ontology* (duty), and *Teleology* (consequence).

The Organization of This Book

As I have mentioned above, the format of this book will be that of the Western ethical tradition, which focuses on (1) the moral agent, or the person as a moral actor; (2) the moral norms, or standards, that guide us; and (3) the consequences, or ultimate outcomes, that result from our actions. And within this framework I believe you will find that the source of morality, the standard of morality, and the goal of morality are found in Christ. Part One, which includes this chapter, will introduce you to ethics in general and to Christian ethics in particular.

Part Two will talk about the moral agent — you. What and who is the human person? Why are we unique as moral beings? What does it mean to be responsible and virtuous? Why is it significant that we are moral agents who live among particular communities in specific times and places?

Part Three will address moral norms, or standards. How is it that people have notions of right and wrong? Where do these standards come from? Is the conscience a faithful standard? What about biblical laws? Are there norms that apply everywhere?

Part Four will address consequences. What are good and what are bad consequences? For whom are they good or bad? When should we be concerned with the consequences of our actions on all other people, or animals, or the environment — now or in the future? What about ultimate consequences such as the Final Judgment, the Second Coming of Christ?

I will use case studies along the way in this book. I will introduce three of them now, and raise them again at various points throughout the book. I do not intend to systematically address each case in each chapter. Rather, I will raise one or another of the cases to your attention when a case is clearly relevant to the subject of a given chapter. Here, in brief, are the case studies.

This book may not answer all of the moral issues that you may have. But my hope is that it will give you the skills and dispositions you need to address them responsibly for yourself.

Case Study (1)

Jeff is a student at a Christian college. He gets decent grades and often attends chapel worship services. He is, of course, "wired" with his own laptop. When he gets home from class or is stressed out for any reason, he will often go to his dorm and look at online porn sites. He doesn't do this every day, but certainly every week. His roommate either doesn't know or does it himself, so there is no risk of being found out.

Case Study (2)

Jerry and Lori are in their mid-forties. They both have had good educations and now have very good jobs. Their kids are in college and have received some prestigious scholarships. Lori owns her own business, and recently it has thrived. They are considering a move to a downtown condominium overlooking the lake. It is an opulent living space and will cost them three times the value of their current house. But it will be nearer to work and will give them a smaller, more manageable space than their house (whose extra rooms for children they don't need anymore).

Case Study (3)

John and Dee are in their fifties. John's mother, Alice, lives in the house John grew up in. It has been six years since John's father died. Alice is starting to show signs of age. She broke her hip last year, and she had a car accident last month that she loudly protests was the other driver's fault, but the police report states otherwise. When Dee visited Alice recently, her refrigerator had a strange collection of condiments, greens, and fruits in it — and the smell was not good. John's siblings live hundreds of miles away.

Ending Questions

1. Is ethics — and especially Christian ethics — necessarily judgmental?
2. Do we have the right to make moral judgments? Why or why not?
3. Is it actually true that non-Christians are more moral than Christians are?
4. The author argues that salvation and morality are two separate categories. Do you agree, and what difference does it make?
5. Can an ethical system that builds on a Greek foundation be Christian?

Works Cited and Further Reading

Crook, Roger H. *An Introduction to Christian Ethics.* Upper Saddle River, NJ: Prentice Hall, 2007.

Grim, Patrick. "Questions of Value." In "The Great Courses: Philosophy and Intellectual History" (a series of recorded lectures). Chantilly, VA: The Teaching Company, 2005.

Hare, John. *Why Bother Being Good? The Place of God in the Moral Life.* Downers Grove, IL: InterVarsity, 2002.

Lovin, Robin. *Christian Ethics: An Essential Guide.* Nashville: Abingdon, 2000.

Maguire, Daniel, and Nicholas Fargnoli. *On Moral Grounds: The Art/Science of Ethics.* New York: Crossroad, 1996.

O'Connell, Timothy E. *Making Disciples.* New York: Crossroad/Herder, 1998.

Pojman, Louis P. *How Should We Live? An Introduction to Ethics.* Belmont, CA: Thomson/Wadsworth, 2005.

CHAPTER TWO

How the Bible Guides Christian Ethics

CHRISTIANS ARE KNOWN as people of the book. We have been formed by Scripture and are re-formed whenever we turn to it again. In this chapter I will explore the dynamic relationship between a Christian and Scripture when the Christian seeks moral guidance from Scripture.

I intentionally did not entitle this chapter "Using the Bible in Christian Ethics." My reason for avoiding that title is that it might give the impression that we stand at some distance from the Bible, and then go to it now and again for bits of moral guidance. That is not the case. Rather, Christians are already deeply embedded within the biblical story. We are part of the community that created the Bible, and our community was itself created by the Word. That community is the church. Thus Christian morality has been established by our participation in the church long before we turn to the Bible for specific moral guidance.

Perhaps it seems obvious to you that Christians should look to the Bible as a moral guide. But the fact that people in twenty-first-century America turn to a diverse set of writings from the Ancient Near East for moral guidance is really quite striking. The Christian Bible has sixty-six "books," written by dozens of authors, many of whom we don't know by name. (Roman Catholic and Orthodox traditions use another thirteen to sixteen books in their canons.) These books are written in languages not commonly spoken, and include histories, dreams, poetry, letters, proverbs, and other forms of literature that often sound strange to modern readers. They were collected by the ancient Hebrews and by members of the early Christian church, who believed that they make up God's inspired Word.

At a foundational level, the fact that we do expect moral guidance from the Bible makes sense, inasmuch as it is the source of basic beliefs about who God is, what the world is, who we are, what the good is, and so on. The Bible sets forth the basic framework on which we build our social world. In other places of the globe, different religious writings, such as the Qur'an (Islam) or the Bhagavad Gita (Hinduism), serve similar roles. These religious classics all provide guidance, giving each faith tradition essential directions about who they are, what the good and the right are, and what things are of ultimate value.

Christians believe that the Bible is God's true and complete revelation, and we also trust that the moral guidance we receive from Scripture is the truest and most complete moral guidance available to us. We trust that God is good, and that Scripture reveals God's goodness and shows God's people how to be good. We see that God set standards and goals for his people in the past, and we believe that since they are grounded in God's own character, they continue to guide us toward Christian morality today.

If you are a Christian, you have probably assumed that the Bible is the main book that guides your morality. But the Bible is not always a clear moral map. It is not an ethics textbook — or, for that matter, an ecology or anthropology textbook — or any other kind of textbook. It tells the story of God's relationship with his people in God's world. Many problems may arise if we try to make the Bible guide our morality in ways that the Bible itself does not intend.

Since it is not an ethics textbook, the Bible does not intend to do — nor should we expect it to do — any of the following:

Terms

The church: the one universal, catholic, and apostolic church that includes all believers throughout time and space; it is sometimes called the "church as organism."

churches: the three main strains of the Christian church — Orthodox, Roman Catholic, and Protestant — that are sometimes referred to as the "institutional church."

Churches: particular denominations, such as the United Methodist Church (in America), or congregations within denominations, such as the First Presbyterian Church of Richland, Michigan.

- provide a set of rules of conduct for us on a case-by-case basis;
- provide us with a seven- or twelve-step plan to morality;
- provide us with a portrait gallery of ideal moral figures;
- provide us with a standardized list of moral principles.

Also, be advised that there is not just one biblical ethic. The ethical principles within the Bible include diverse rules, virtues, goals, models, and so on. And the church has taken up these diverse themes and interpreted them in many different ways in the course of Christian history. For example, while they were a persecuted minority in the Roman Empire, Christians emphasized virtues such as hospitality and patient endurance. When the church later became the leader of that empire, it emphasized other virtues, such as courage and respect for authority.

I should clear up a term or two. "Biblical ethics" usually refers to the ethics that are found in the Bible; that is, it describes the ethics that an individual biblical author espouses. These ethics may be seen in the actions and attitudes of the biblical characters, or they may be in specific ethical instructions found in some texts. For example, when Joseph refused to have sex with Potiphar's wife, he showed that he would not place temporary pleasure above the vision that God had for his future. On the other hand, when Abraham had sex with his wife's maid in order to have offspring, he showed a willingness to follow local customs *(ethos)* regarding concubines instead of maintaining fidelity to God's promise.

Biblical ethics is the study of morality in the Bible. But in the Bible, moral norms, virtues, and desired consequences develop over time. Consider Jesus' teaching in the Sermon on the Mount, where he says, "You have heard it said," and then quotes a passage from earlier Scripture, the Hebrew Bible. He then says, "But I say to you . . . ," shifting the meaning or bringing out a fuller significance of what was said in the Old Testament. Clearly, Jesus' ethics develop with and expand on the older ethics found in Hebrew Scripture. And even within the Old

Current News

Recently a number of writers have argued that religion has a very negative effect on society. For example, Richard Dawkins argues in *The God Delusion* that belief in God is responsible for many if not most ills in society. What do you think?

Testament itself, the ethics sometimes shift. Consider this teaching on slavery in Exodus:

> When you acquire a Hebrew slave, he shall serve six years; in the seventh year he shall go free, without payment. (Exod. 21:2)

Now compare this verse to the following one in Leviticus:

> If your kinsman under you continues in straits and must give himself over to you, do not subject him to the treatment of a slave. . . . Such male and female slaves as you may have — it is from the nations round about you that you may acquire male and female slaves. (Lev. 25:39, 44)

In the Exodus text, the Israelites could hold other Hebrews as their slaves, though they were to be set free in the Sabbatical year. But in the second and later text, a Hebrew could not hold his fellow kinsman (a Hebrew) as a slave at all; only foreigners could be slaves. So within the Old Testament itself, there is a developing tradition on this moral issue.

The term "Christian ethics" does not refer to the ethics as described in the Bible but to the ethics that Christians at various times and places have developed while often using the Bible as guide. Christian ethics is ongoing. Wherever there are Christians, they attempt to live morally and develop ethical systems to guide them. Christians are found in diverse cultures and times, and these new situations require new ethical thinking. For example, I attended a conference on technology and business ethics in the city of Dalian, China, in 2007. The issues in business ethics that were addressed there would not have arisen anywhere a century ago, since the technology did not exist until recently. And the conference would not have occurred in China until at least 1990, when China opened itself to free-market reforms. So people continue to encounter new moral issues, as well as old ones in new settings. As cultures develop in new ways, Christian ethics must also adapt and grow.

While it can be hazardous to use Scripture for moral guidance, it is quite proper for Christians to read Scripture as a moral guide. Providing moral guidance is not the Bible's only task, but showing disciples how to "do justice, love mercy, and walk humbly before our God" (Micah 6:8) is certainly central to the intent of the biblical writers.

As we turn to Scripture for moral guidance, we find that it speaks to us in a variety of ways. Although that variety is in one sense almost limitless, I will summarize the kinds of guidance it provides under the following five categories:

1. Scripture provides moral norms/standards.
2. Scripture encourages and animates virtue.
3. Scripture provides us with analogues.
4. Scripture shows us the way of wisdom.
5. Scripture shows us God's own concerns and invites us to share in them.

Moral Norms

The first thing that Scripture does is give us *moral standards*, or moral norms — that is, standards of moral behavior. (They are the subject of the third major section of this book, so I will wait until that point to describe the kinds of norms found in Scripture.) For now, I will briefly speak of how biblical norms serve as a guide for Christians.

There are clearly many standards for behavior in Scripture. Many of them come to us in the form of law codes like those found in Exodus, Leviticus, and Deuteronomy. Large sections of prophetic literature also refer to these laws. And Jesus himself not only kept the law but deepened its meaning and fulfilled its intent.

Notice the role that the law plays in the life of God's people. When the law is given to Israel, it is *after* Israel is delivered from slavery. So the law is clearly not the condition that God established for Israel's salvation, but a consequence of that salvation. In other words, living up to the standards of the law does not save us; but those who are saved should live up to the standards of the law. The law was given to Israel — and is given to Christians — for three reasons: first, to show us that we need a Savior, since we cannot keep the law ourselves (Rom. 7:7-25); second, to establish a basis for a just society (Deut. 4:5-8); and third, to demonstrate ways in which believers can show love for God and others (John 14:15-21).

Many Christians see obedience to the law as the heart of Christian ethics. An old hymn, "Trust and Obey," makes this point. This is a pretty straightforward ethic: God commands, and we do what is commanded. At one level this is certainly true. God says, "Do not steal." So don't! If you do, you have done moral wrong (sin) and must cease and repent. Much of our moral life can certainly be guided in this way. We really don't need to ask many more questions. God commands that we do not commit adultery, kill, steal, and so forth — and thus we must not do those things.

Trust and Obey

When we walk with the Lord
In the light of his Word,
What a glory he sheds on our way!
While we do his good will,
He abides with us still,
And with those who will trust and obey.
Trust and obey,
For there's no other way
To be happy in Jesus,
But to trust and obey.

Yet questions arise with this approach. Which laws are we to obey — the Ten Commandments, the Law of Love, Paul's statement that women should wear veils and not have authority over men? Does God still command all of these things?

Not only do Christians believe that God's written law will direct us in the correct path; most also seek guidance from the living Word, or Spirit. Thus we find God's will for our lives not only by looking up applicable laws in the Bible but also by carefully listening for the Spirit of God as we walk before him. Many believe that the method of turning to specific Bible verses to draw out principles for contemporary moral issues can be a literalist and faulty approach. Thus they urge us to listen for the leading of God's Spirit in the moments of our decision-making.

There is support for this spiritual emphasis. It is true that we are already embedded in the community created by the Bible, and we are attuned to the voice of the Spirit, the Spirit of Christ, as it leads the church. And since we are a *communion* of believers, it is not just one individual who is led by the Spirit, but believers as a whole gathered in worship who hear the Spirit's murmurs. Thus, listening to the Spirit as it guides us from day to day is an immediate and dynamic way of doing ethics.

However, questions also arise about this approach:

1. Why does God seem not to speak to us in some times of moral difficulty, or at least not very clearly?
2. How does the leading of the Spirit relate to the words of Scripture that are available to us?
3. How do we judge whether what we heard was from the Spirit of God?

The validity of the first question is supported by experience. Haven't you had a time in which you wondered what you should do — but didn't have a clear spiritual direction about what it was? The second question is valid as well: God does not contradict himself. If the written Word is saying "ABC," the Spirit cannot be whispering "XYZ." The third question is also important. Too often some Christians have done strange and even horrible things after claiming they were led by the Spirit. Nations have even gone to war believing that God was on their side. Claiming spiritual direction can be perilous.

Seeing scriptural law as a moral guide raises the issue of historical relevance. The laws of Scripture were written in a particular society for a particular people. We live in a different society and among a different community. How shall we relate the laws from that earlier community to our own? What about new cases that were clearly unforeseen by earlier texts? Related to this issue is the argument that simple obedience leaves little room for personal creativity and virtue. It seems that a computer or a dog could be a good Christian in this sense. God says do A, and I do A. Then I look up the law for situation B and do that.

Historical Tidbit

In World War II the soldiers of the German *Wehrmacht* (regular army) had the declaration *"Gott mit uns"* engraved on their belt buckles. It means "God is with *us*."

Scripture Encourages and Animates Virtue

The second way Christians often use Scripture for moral guidance is to form their character. The issue here is not "What shall I do?" but "Who shall I become?'" In chapter 5, I will address virtue in more detail. Here I wish to show that the Bible is in fact a good source for discovering and developing virtue. A well-known passage in Galatians talks about virtue under the heading of "Fruits of the Spirit": "But the fruit of the Spirit is love, joy, peace, patience, kindness, goodness, faithfulness, gentleness, and self-control . . ." (Gal. 5:22-23).

Revelation Is Not Magic

Some believers today attempt to learn the will of God by consulting mediums or having their fortune read. In many countries, Christians believe that shamans or spiritists can put them in touch with the dead or with spiritual powers. Scripture resolutely condemns these attempts to get to know the spirit world in these ways. The ways to know God and his will are to be with fellow spiritual believers who seek God in prayer and meditation on Scripture.

A Christian disciple is by definition one who follows Christ. By examining Scripture, we learn the ways in which Christ lived by observing his virtues. In fact, one brief definition of Christian ethics could be this: to let Christ's virtue live through us. Seeing the Bible as a guide to virtue and living by what it says is a way of doing this. In Scripture it is not only Jesus who shows us how to live virtuously. He is certainly the ideal model of virtue, but throughout Scripture we are encouraged to develop virtues that are appropriate for the faithful. At various points we are called to be fearless, humble, industrious, self-sacrificial, and so on. Virtues permit us to live in a way that is appropriate to our surroundings.

But this approach to biblical ethics also has its problems. There may be cases in which it is not clear what even a virtuous person should do. Or we may not be sure which of the virtues is most relevant to our situation. Or we may be blind to the fact that we are participants in some vices of our culture. And, in general, virtues are very general. We might all agree that justice is a virtue, but doing justice in your particular setting could be very hard to discern.

Scripture Provides Us with Analogies

The third way we are directed by Scripture is by example, model, or analogy ("analogy" comes from the Greek *ana* [along] and *logos* [word]; so, literally, an analogue is two words alongside each other). There are some excellent examples of faithfulness — and unfaithfulness — in

Scripture. Acting like Abraham or Ruth or Mary or Jesus is a good goal to have. These were people who followed God and were recognized for it. Educators tell us that role-modeling is an excellent teaching technique, and Scripture provides us with both positive and negative models. Perhaps the struggle you face is similar to one faced by a character in Scripture. How did that person handle such a situation? How does the Bible judge what that person did?

But using this approach also raises the issue of time and culture. Jesus was a first-century Jewish craftsman. You and I live two thousand years later and in a very different culture, one that uses different languages and has many different experiences than did Jesus' culture. Therefore, asking what Jesus would do about nuclear war, or genetic engineering, or computer pornography becomes a rather speculative question. We have little data in Scripture about these things in Jesus' life from which to draw.

Another limitation is the fact that the biblical characters themselves are dramatically flawed. Take Abraham, for example. He is certainly a model of faith when he leaves home and family to follow God; but he is also a model of cowardliness and deceit when he tells Pharaoh that Sarah is his sister, not his wife.

Scripture Shows Us the Way of Wisdom

Wisdom is another way that Scripture guides us. Much biblical literature in both the Old and New Testaments is called "Wisdom literature." In this literature we do not find commands such as those in the law codes, but depictions of how things should go on earth. Scripture presents two "ways" of life, and Psalm 1 is a beautiful example of this:

> Happy is the man who has not followed the counsel of the wicked,
>   or taken the path of sinners,
>   or joined the company of the insolent.
>   Rather, the teaching of the LORD is his delight,
>   and he studies that teaching day and night.

[Handwritten margin note: What would Jesus do, → What is the theme or heart behind what Jesus does?]

He is like a tree planted beside streams of water,
>   which yields its fruit in season,
>   whose foliage never fades,
>   and whatever it produces thrives.
Not so the wicked;
>   rather, they are like chaff that wind blows away.
Therefore the wicked will not survive judgment,
>   nor sinners in the assembly of the righteous;
For the LORD cherishes the way of the righteous,
>   but the way of the wicked is doomed.

Notice that Psalm 1 is descriptive. It tells us about two possible paths we might take. The path that the righteous follow is based on the word of God; it endures, and it leads to a life of blessing. The path of the wicked, in contrast, will lead to futility and destruction.

Wisdom literature occurs throughout the world. In fact, there are direct parallels between some Wisdom literature in the Old Testament and Egyptian wisdom literature of the same time period. This should not surprise us. Wisdom literature shows us how life works throughout the world. Wherever people are industrious, honest, and careful, they tend to prosper. Those who are self-indulgent, dishonest, and careless tend to self-destruct. This is as true today as it was in ancient Palestine or Egypt. Wisdom literature is not a series of laws that tell you whether or not you may do something; rather, it is a depiction of the way things tend to go. It shows us how to live in harmony with our neighbors and with nature. When we read Wisdom texts in Scripture, we are not told specifically what to do; rather, we are directed on a particular path. Many of Jesus' teachings in the parables are also Wisdom sayings.

A potential limitation of biblical Wisdom literature as an approach to moral guidance is its vagueness. We may all agree that a path of moderation or faithfulness generally leads to prosperity and happiness. But what constitutes moderation or faithfulness for us here and now? How, for

A Wisdom Teaching of Jesus

"Therefore, everyone who hears these words of mine and puts them into practice is like a wise man who built his house on the rock. The rain came down, the streams rose, and the winds blew and beat against that house; yet it did not fall, because it had its foundation on the rock."
(Matt. 7:24-25)

example, does a career choice we make today "build on the rock"? Or will wisdom for a person with your character be different for a person with my character?

Scripture Shows Us God's Own Concerns

The last way that Scripture informs us is by showing us where the heart of God lies. What is God constantly doing, and for whom? As many liberation theologians have pointed out, the heart of God tends to favor the poor and the outcast. God loves the younger son, the infertile wife, the poor, the alien, the widow, and so on. All of these were people on the margins of society in the Ancient Near East, where the oldest son received the inheritance, the fertile woman was blessed, the rich prospered, and the adult male citizen had rights. Jesus picks up the theme of God's special concern for the marginalized at the inauguration of his ministry. In Luke 4:18-19 he says: "The Spirit of the Lord is upon me, because he has anointed me to announce good news to the poor, proclaim freedom to the prisoners and recovery of sight to the blind, to release the oppressed, to proclaim the year of the Lord's favor."

Feminist theologians have recently elevated the status of women in Christianity as well. Although the gospel was written in ancient times, when patriarchy (male rule) was the law, the gospel is capable of equalizing the power between men and women. For example, in Galatians 3:28, Paul says, "There is no longer Jew or Greek, there is no longer slave or free, there is no longer male and female; for all of you are one in Christ Jesus." Clearly Paul could distinguish between males and females, Jews and Greeks. But he makes these human distinctions relative, placing them below the one distinction that matters most: whether a person is found in Christ Jesus. Theologians who do this today are following the pattern set out in Scripture. Human qualifications

Case Study

Does the Bible say anything at all about Jerry and Lori buying a lakefront condo? Clearly not, at least not in a direct way. But what about analogies in Scripture? Did anyone in Scripture do something self-indulgent and then regret it, or choose to live modestly and gain from it? Is it wise to take on that level of debt? Positively speaking, perhaps the couple could use the extra profit from Lori's business to do something that would directly benefit the needy.

that create social divisions along sexual, racial, and class lines are false standards. The great standard was set for us in Christ Jesus, and those who are his disciples must cast off false ones. When we listen to the Bible in this way, we hear God calling us to stand with the poor, the outcast, and the stranger. Thus an ethic that focuses on this aspect of biblical teaching would ask, "How will my actions affect the poor?" or "Whose side am I taking on this issue — that of the privileged or that of the underprivileged?"

Conclusion

Because the Bible speaks to us with many voices, we need to listen with skillfully tuned ears. We can see the norms, the analogies, the wisdom, the virtues, and the concerns that are there. By studying the texts, their contexts, their genres, and so forth, we can understand more and more what the Word is saying to us, and how it is guiding us into moral discernment.

Ending Questions

1. Is the idea that there are many forms of biblical and Christian ethics disconcerting? Is it true?
2. Can you think of other places in Scripture where you see ethical development?
3. Are there more ways that the Bible provides us with moral guidance than the five mentioned in this chapter?
4. Why is the fact that the law was given after the deliverance from Egypt (the Exodus) important?
5. How do you determine which of the biblical laws are still applicable?
6. Has the leading of the Holy Spirit been a moral guide in your life, and should biblical figures be used as moral examples? Always?

Works Cited and Further Reading

Fowl, Stephen, and L. Gregory Jones. *Reading in Communion: Scripture and Ethics in Christian Life*. Grand Rapids: Eerdmans, 1991.

Hauerwas, Stanley. "The Moral Authority of Scripture: The Politics and Ethics of Remembering." In *Readings in Moral Theology,* edited by Charles E. Curran and Richard A. McCormick. New York: Paulist Press, 1978.

Kelsey, David. *The Uses of Scripture in Recent Theology*. Philadelphia: Fortress, 1975.

Ogletree, Thomas W. *The Use of the Bible in Christian Ethics: A Constructive Essay*. Philadelphia: Fortress, 1983.

Siker, Jeffrey. *Scripture and Ethics: Twentieth-Century Portraits*. New York: Oxford University Press, 1997.

Spohn, William C. *What Are They Saying about Scripture and Ethics?* New York: Paulist Press, 1995.

Verhey, Allen. "The Use of Scripture in Ethics." In *Readings in Moral Theology,* edited by Charles E. Curran and Richard A. McCormick. New York: Paulist Press, 1978.

Character

CHAPTER THREE

The Moral Agent

AT THIS POINT it's important to give a definition of a moral agent. A moral agent is someone who is responsible and responsive to himself/ herself, to God and other beings, and to creation; he/she is accountable to a moral standard and can foresee potential results of his/her actions.

The Bible does not offer proof that people are morally responsible and responsive to one another, to the environment, and to God. The Bible assumes it. In fact, the very first story of human-divine interaction is a moral test: "'You may eat from any tree in the garden,' God told the man, 'except from the tree of the knowledge of good and evil; the day you eat from that, you are surely doomed to die'" (Gen. 2:16-17). In this first story the Bible assumes that humans can — or at least could — choose the right. All normal humans are moral agents; a Christian moral agent is one who recognizes that we are related to God as children of God, to other persons as brothers and sisters, and to creation as fellow creatures.

It is crucial to set forth what it means to be a responsible agent when developing a moral system. As the Catholic ethicist Richard Gula puts it, "In a nutshell, morality is about what we should do because of who we are" (Gula, 24). In this section on the moral agent, I will explore the way humans relate and respond morally to God, others, and animals/nature. First, I will describe the ways in which theologians and philosophers have understood the human person; second, I will explain how our degree of responsibility can grow or diminish; and third, I will show ways in which our communities shape us as moral agents.

God's Special and Physical Creatures

In order to understand who we are as moral agents, we turn to the biblical story of creation. Humans were created from the earth's matter (Gen. 2:7) and continue to live as material beings. Upon dying, these bodies will again become lifeless chemicals. But on being resurrected, we will be reunited with a resurrection body. This complete and everlasting connection to our physical selves means not only that we *have* bodies but that we *are* bodies. This flesh-self puts us in a permanent and special relationship to the physical world. The fact that we are physical creatures is not the cause of evil, but rather a good aspect of our selves. Our physical aspect provides us with crucial characteristics and limitations. We are either male or female; we are short or tall; we are brown, black, or white. Our physical self means that none of us can be in two places at once; none of us can live for more than about 120 years; and none of us will turn out to be cats. Our physical aspect means that we will all grow old and die.

The great Greek philosophers such as Plato thought that having a physical body was the source of human problems. They thought it would be better by far to have pure reason that could detach itself from the chaotic desires and continuous needs of the body. Platonists had a saying: *soma sema*. The *soma* is the "body" (we get words such as "psychosomatic" from *soma*); *sema* means "prison." Thus Platonists saw the corruptible body as the prison of the more noble reason, or soul.

Christian faith has also often adopted this negative Platonic attitude toward our bodies. But this negativity is not to be found in Scripture. Certainly we are to avoid sin, and Saint Paul sometimes used the Greek term for flesh, *sarx,* when he spoke of sin. But, according to Scripture, the human body is good — in fact, "very good." Take, for example, Genesis 1:26-27:

Then God said, "Let us make humankind in our image, according to our likeness; and let them have dominion over the fish of the sea, and over the birds of the air, and over the cattle, and over all the wild animals of the earth, and over every creeping thing that creeps upon the earth." So God created humankind in his image, in the image of God he created them; male and female he created them.

Humans are described as being created in the "image and likeness" of God. The words *image* and *likeness* are not philosophical terms that attempt to explain the structure of human nature; rather, they show that among all the creatures of the earth, humans are those who most resemble God, relate most directly to him, and take up God's tasks. It is not only one particular characteristic such as having souls that makes us images of God. It is the fact that we are created to be God's representatives on earth. God placed us here to extend his benevolent rule over the earth.

Philosophers and theologians have strained over the meaning of the "image and likeness of God" for centuries. Some have argued that we retained the image of God after the first sin, but lost the likeness. Others have argued that the spiritual nature was lost in sin, but is restored after conversion. But such attempts to define the image of God as being one aspect of our nature can lead to abuse. Problems arise if we define what constitutes a human being on the basis of one particular characteristic, because we can then deny some people the status of human beings by claiming that they do not possess that characteristic. For example, the conquistadors of Latin America assumed that humans were unique because they had rational souls. They did not believe that American Indians had souls, and thus thought that they were free to kill the Amerindians as if they were animals. They were wrong. There is a danger to any such re-

> "It is a serious thing . . . to remember that the dullest and most uninteresting person you talk to may one day be a creature which, if you saw it now, you would be strongly tempted to worship, or else a horror and a corruption such as you now meet, if at all, only in a nightmare. All day long we are, in some degree, helping each other to one or the other of these destinations. It is in the light of these overwhelming possibilities, it is with the awe and the circumspection proper to them, that we should conduct all our dealings with one another, all friendships, all loves, all play, all politics. . . . It is immortals whom we joke with, work with, marry, snub, and exploit — immortal horrors or everlasting splendors."
>
> C. S. Lewis, "The Weight of Glory"

ductionism — that is, that we are only our genetics, or our reason, or our chemistry, or our capacity to earn. One group of humans cannot set the standard of what humanity is for another. Instead, it is the fact that God calls us into relationship with himself that establishes the baseline of human nature for all.

Humans have a crucial role to play within creation. Our role is to be caretakers of God's earth. God gave humankind "dominion" over nature so that we might act responsibly within God's world on his behalf. Our first divinely assigned task is to "cultivate" the place we have been given (Gen. 2:15). "Cultivating," or "tilling" (from the Hebrew *avad*), is an agricultural term. Our task shows that, though the world is good, we are not to leave its resources untouched; we are to develop its potential so that its productivity is unleashed for the common good. Like our heavenly Father, in whose image we are created, we are creative. We can think and build, imagine and draw, reflect and write. God is the Creator, and like him we are re-creators who take some aspect of creation and develop it in such a way that God's world is enhanced.

The second term from God's job description for humans in Genesis 2:15 is the one we translate as "keep," or "care for." It is derived from the Hebrew term *shamar,* and it has the connotation of guarding, revering, and protecting. As examples, the Ten Commandments tell us to *shamar* the Sabbath (Deut. 5:12), and the priests were told to *shamar* the tabernacle (Num. 1:53). This term shows that we humans are in charge of and have responsibility for creation. We are to guard the sanctity of the world. We are not only to be productive and fruitful on God's earth, but we are also to serve as its guardians, protecting and watching over it. We are to cultivate and keep the earth as if God were doing it himself. This may be the concept behind the third petition of the Lord's Prayer: "Thy will be done, on earth as it is in heaven."

We perform our divinely appointed tasks within unique relationships to God, other persons, and creation. These relationships can be characterized by indifference, hatred, or love. We may resent God's rule over us and the world; we may not care whether God is there. Or we may respond in gratitude to the offer of life that God makes to us in creation and again in Christ. So we may respond to others in the same way. How should we respond to others who are also God's image-bearers? The answer in Scripture is direct and well known: "You shall love them as yourself" (Lev. 19:18). This norm of love is the one we were created to embody, and it sums up the standard of morality to which we are called.

One person did show perfect human morality: Jesus, who was also the Son of God. He is both the model for humanity and the originator of a new humanity. He was completely human and morally perfect. By taking on human nature, he made it what it should be. He did not take on the nature of a dog, or a lizard, or a geranium. He became a human being, one who was made in the image and likeness of God so that he could renew the human image. To image God on earth required that God become one of his own kind; and Jesus is still one of our kind. He now reigns at the right hand of God as a king fully human and fully divine. Our nature — that is, human nature — is now perfected in the heavens with God. It is this Christ-like nature that is both the source of our life with God and our goal.

To conclude this section on what makes humans God's special creatures, I should note something that I have mentioned but perhaps not emphasized enough. What makes us special creatures is the fact that we belong to God. In other words, it may not be nearly as important to say *what* we are as it is to know *whose* we are. A Reformation-era catechism asks and answers a significant question:

Q. What is your only comfort in life and in death?

A. That I, with body and soul, both in life and death, am not my own,
    but belong to my faithful Savior Jesus Christ.
    (*Heidelberg Catechism,* Q & A 1)

This is a good answer. Who we are depends on whose we are, and the fact that we belong to one who loves us beyond measure is comfort indeed.

Morally Responsive and Responsible Creatures

What must you know, or do, or feel, and how much of it must you know, or do, or feel in order to be a responsible moral agent? To answer this question, I turn to an important American theologian of the twentieth century, H. Richard Niebuhr. In his book *The Responsible Self,* Niebuhr claims that there are three criteria for responsibility:

- The responsible self can initiate action.
- The responsible self can respond, not merely react.
- The responsible self can account for or explain her actions.

Allow me to add two more criteria that are implicit in Niebuhr's work:

- The responsible agent knows of a moral standard for her actions.
- The responsible agent can foresee potential outcomes of her actions.

Let's explore these criteria one by one.

First, a responsible self is one who can initiate action. When the sun is bright, our pupils get smaller to allow in less light; when there is little light, they dilate to let in more. These are reactions that we have, not actions that we initiate. A moral agent can not only experience things, but interpret them and act accordingly. For example, if I interpret the light in my room as being too faint to read by, I will initiate the action of turning on a lamp. The physical response that my eyes had to the fading sunlight was not something I initiated, but turning on the lamp was.

Second, my response to a situation is one that I interpret and then respond to, not merely react to. I respond within my own context and frame of interpretation. If a driver whom I recognize as the local auto-body repairman cuts me off on the highway, I might interpret it as an attempt on his part to drum up business. Or I might simply assume that he needed to get off the highway at that exit. The driver and I then respond within this context. Moral actions must be responses interpreted within a context, not merely physical or emotive reactions.

Third, the driver of the car that cuts me off is morally responsible and must be able to account for his actions. No, he was not hoping to cause a crash that would bring business, but he did in fact need to exit the highway at that point.

Fourth, the other driver must know that there are norms in place. Indeed, speed and lane changes are regulated by law. He must know that there is some moral — and in this case, legal — standard for his action. This is not to say that he must know and understand every law related to all of his actions; nor does he have to read the great philosophers on the subject in question. Rather, he must simply be aware that questions of right and wrong or of good and evil are present. In the terms used in chapter 1, the driver and I must know that there is a question of morality present.

Finally, the driver must know that a sudden lane change can have consequences. We all must have some knowledge of the potential results of our actions. For example, if I throw a stone, I must know what is below me in the trajectory of the toss. If I throw a stone from a bridge, I must know that it could potentially harm someone who is passing below. If I fail to look over the edge of the bridge, I am being irresponsible, since I not only don't know what damage might occur, but I choose not to find out. Here's another example: I'm informed that having sex has the potential result of making a baby. So if I have sex, I need to recognize and take responsibility for this potential result if I am to be a responsible person.

The example of the careless driver is simple. But many moral responses are complex and profound. How do you respond to the physical report that says you are now pregnant? Into what kind of interpretive frame do you put that information? How have you understood incidents related to this in the past? Or how should a political leader like President Obama interpret and respond to the actions of rebels in Libya against their forty-year dictator, Muammar al-Qaddafi? Does he commit the U.S. planes to make airstrikes against the Qaddafi loyalists and in favor of the rebels? What could be some potential results? In none of the cases mentioned — the driver, the pregnancy, or the U.S. airstrikes — is the agent merely a reactor who is compelled by nature to do one and only one thing, such as the eye is when it encounters light. We are more than reactors; we are responsible responders.

What about my dog? Is she a responsible moral agent? She seems to know something about what is right and wrong: for example, don't bite people or other animals, don't leave the yard, don't soil the carpet. She usually obeys these rules, but sometimes she doesn't. Does this ability to obey or disobey make her a moral agent? I think not. Let's evaluate her morality on the standards that Niebuhr and I have set forth.

Can my dog initiate action? Yes, in a way she can. If the sunlight is too bright and warm for her, she moves to a place where she can lie in the shade. But this is only the reaction of a mammal that is experiencing too much heat for her body. Does she know that there are standards for her behavior? It's true that she might know these standards, but that's only because I trained her with them. In theory, I could have trained her in very different norms, for example, to bite the neighbors, run wildly through the neighborhood, and soil the carpet. She only knows the standards for her behavior because I taught them to her. She doesn't knowingly choose one standard over another, so she can't be held morally responsible for the standards chosen for her.

Next, does my dog see the consequences of her actions? Not really. She just knows that if she soils the carpet, she might be banished to the basement; but she only reacts to the fear of punishment or the good feeling of praise for good behavior. Can she account for her actions? No, she explains nothing. I might be able to explain why I think she did something, but she cannot. She does not reason; rather, she reacts in line with her instinct. If given the chance, she will kill squirrels or rabbits. Her nature compels her to do so. She can't develop the virtues of patience and peacefulness when it comes to squirrels.

Does she see the likely consequences of her behavior? This is a bit harder to say. Can she foresee that she will be banished to the basement if she soils the floor? I doubt it. But could she still know she ought not to soil the floor? Somehow, perhaps yes. Still, all in all, my dog lacks some of the capabilities that moral action requires. Although she is a dear creature to me, she is not a responsible moral agent.

Case Study

How can John and Dee, whom we first met in chapter 1, be responsible about John's mother, Alice? They face a number of difficult issues. Is Alice still a human person? Or if she is today, how long will she be one? Alice's sister Jenny is now completely senile. She doesn't recognize her own children. Maybe John and Dee have to be the responsible agents for their mother as her capacities diminish. But how will they treat her most humanely? Should she move in with them, or should she go to a rest home? How can they treat this diminishing human with dignity, yet handle her growing physical needs?

Particular Responsibilities of the Moral Agent

All people are created in God's image and are in relationship with him, with other persons, and with creatures and creation. But we may have greater or lesser responsibility to particular people, creatures, and aspects of creation at different times and in different situations. What causes the changes in levels of responsibility?

Special knowledge is one reason that some people are more responsible than others. For example, my wife is a nurse who teaches CPR. She knows how to help people who are wounded or sick. I, on the other hand, have a very limited knowledge of medicine. So if we were riding along in our car and an accident occurred directly ahead of us, her responsibility to the injured would be greater than mine. Lack of knowledge is an obvious impediment to responsible action. My knowing little about medicine precludes me from doing much good in the case of an emergency. But it isn't wrong that I don't know how to care for the injured; it's simply one of the many things I don't have knowledge about. We can't know everything, and we're not responsible for everything. If that were true, we'd be God.

Another criterion that determines our level of responsibility is our freedom. In the example above, I was free to throw a stone from a bridge. This seems fairly obvious. No one was forcing me to throw it, and I was completely capable of doing so or refraining from doing so. But there are other kinds of freedoms and limitations. All of us, for example, need food and water. So while we may be free to turn down dessert after tonight's dinner, we are not free to reject all food and drink for very long. Our freedom is limited, in part, by our nature. I am not free to jump and dunk a basketball; my stature and lack of jumping ability limit me. I am not free to speak Chinese as a native speaker, since I was not born in China. Our circumstances and our nature limit our freedom. Again, there's nothing wrong with being limited; it's simply part of who we are.

A Legal Case Regarding Dogs

There was a case in California in which two large dogs were left in the stairwell of an apartment complex. Those dogs killed a young woman who was trying to get into her apartment. The dogs were euthanized, and the owners of the dogs were given significant jail time. What does this tell you about the responsibility of the dogs, as well as that of the owners? Do you agree with the judgment?

The Moral Agent

The moral agent must be both responsive and responsible.

She must respond to God, others, and her environment.

She must know the relevant norms and possible outcomes of her actions, and be free to choose her actions.

She must be able to give some account of her actions.

Our freedom can also be limited by coercion. If a man hijacks me and my car and says, "You'll be the getaway driver for us, or I'll kill you," I would quickly sense that my choices are limited. I suppose I do have the choice to refuse, but since that entails the end of my earthly existence, it really isn't a free choice. Civil law recognizes this when it speaks of doing something under duress, or of being coerced. I couldn't be convicted of any crime in this robbery because I wouldn't be a free participant in it. To be free, I must be the actor, not the instrument of someone else's action.

Our degree of responsibility is also dependent on the degree of power that we have. For example, the CEO of a company is responsible for fraud in the company in a way that the mailroom worker is not. He or she has greater responsibility and thus greater culpability. In addition, we have some responsibility as parts of greater entities. For example, I am a member of a church. It may be that my church decides to buy land, or discipline a member, or start a ministry among street children. As a part of that church, I have some (though limited) responsibility for what the church does. Clearly, in the case of both the company and the church, the officers of these institutions have the most responsibility, but if we are part of something, we must share responsibility for it to some degree. This is called corporate responsibility.

There are three options for being responsible that parallel the three options for being moral. We saw in chapter 1 that actions could be moral, amoral, or immoral. You will recall that amorality has no condition of morality to it, and immorality has the characteristic of being opposed to moral standards. In the same way, we can be responsible or *not responsible,* and responsible or *irresponsible.* For example, if a tornado strikes my town, I have no responsibility for the fact that it happened. But once the tornado hits, I am responsible for what happens to me and others nearby. If I don't act for my good and theirs, I have become irresponsible.

Limitations on the Moral Agent's Responsibility

There are impediments to responsibility. The Roman Catholic tradition is clear on what these include: ignorance, passion, force, and fear. These impediments do not make us amoral; rather, they make us less responsible. (Keep in mind that I am now using the term *moral* as compared to *immoral,* not *amoral.*) *Ignorance* is a fairly straightforward limitation to responsibility. If you don't know that a tornado hit a town, you can't do much for the victims afterward. If you don't know, due to your social context, that borrowing something for a long time is seen as theft in another context, your actions are excusable.

In most Catholic moral teaching, *passion* was also thought to be an impediment to morality (perhaps this idea was derived from the Greek philosophy that I mentioned earlier). Seeing passion as an impediment implies that our emotions can get out of hand and must be ruled by reason. Indeed, we do sometimes react unreasonably. Psychological vulnerabilities from depression or mania can impede our freedom. But the idea that passion is an impediment to morality has two problems. First, passions always have an object or goal. For example, I might be passionate about learning to play second base, or getting a good score on the GRE. Are these things bad? Clearly not. The problem with passions is that they can sometimes serve the wrong goals. For example, you may have a passion for physical pleasure, and you may satisfy that passion by indulging in food, alcohol, or sex. You may have a passion for power or control that you let play out in manipulating or deceiving people. Passion or fervor for something is not in itself wrong; rather, the things we are passionate about can make it wrong.

Corporate Responsibility

Corporate responsibility is the responsibility each of us has as a result of our social location. If we belong to groups — political, economic, religious, familial, and so on — we share in the responsibility for what these groups do.

The second problem with viewing passion as evil derives from recent studies in psychology suggesting that, in fact, it may be a lack of passion that makes us immoral. For instance, a psychopath is someone who has no feelings of remorse. The psychopath may intellectually agree with the notion that murder is wrong, but nevertheless feels no sympathy for his victims. In this case it is a lack of passion that brings about evil. The issue, then, seems not to be the presence of passion but the nature of the passion in question. Love is, in part, a passion. And love for another person should lead to the promotion of the good of that person. Good passion is the source of good morality, not an impediment to it. It is true that certain passions can become twisted, but deep emotional commitment is the basis for good morality.

Fear is also an impediment to moral responsibility. For example, I may choose not to walk through a certain neighborhood out of fear that I could be harmed. But choosing to avoid that neighborhood means that I cannot do any direct moral good there either. It may also be the case that I am under the power of irrational fears. I may fear that there are trolls under the bridge, and thus be unable to help the child who fell into the water below. Everyone has fears. Reasonable or not, they inhibit our range of action.

Earlier I mentioned the issue of force as a limitation on responsibility when I spoke about the carjacking. We cannot be responsible for something we were forced to do. We must have freedom. When we are free and in control of our passions and fears, then we are responsible for our actions and can be held culpable for wrong or evil actions — and can be praised for good and right actions.

Christians may also (falsely) claim that there are two other impediments to their actions: the devil made me do it, or God predestined me to do it. Neither of these claims will stand up to scrutiny. The Bible says that the devil may tempt a person, but the devil cannot cause a person's action. And the great weight of biblical morality holds God's children up as responsible beings. If this were not the case, God would not have made moral norms for his people and created us with the freedom to respond. We would be puppets on strings.

Does being reasonable equal being moral?

Couldn't a lack of passion — apathy — be as grave a flaw as an abundance of passion?

Sometimes people claim that they are not responsible for their actions because of their social location. For example, a child raised in a poor home with an abusive parent may claim that he is not responsible for shooting his teacher. While there is undoubtedly a social plot within which our life stories are played out, it is our own role that we enact and for which we are responsible. This means that we genuinely deserve punishment for the evil and praise for the good that we do. Just as you would praise a musician for a fine performance, you should praise someone who does moral good. We wouldn't say to the musician, "Oh, musicians like you are the beneficiaries of genetic abilities and excellent training, so your performance was nothing praiseworthy." So, too, we should recognize that morally good deeds are not the automatic results of genetics or training.

Suffering may be a limitation on our responsibility as well, though this is not specifically mentioned in the context above. We become more vulnerable and less capable when we suffer. If we suffer physically, we are less capable of movement and action. If we suffer emotionally, we are less capable of responding to others in family and society. Pain itself may cause us to so turn inward that we can do little for others. In these cases it is the responsibility of others to do good for us.

Moral responsibility is a range, not an absolute category, so it is quite possible that we have more responsibility in some cases and less in others. Take homicide, for example. In all homicides, the end result is the same — a human corpse. But the law distinguishes responsibility — and thus culpability — on the basis of the knowledge and freedom of the one who caused the death. To be *culpable* means that one is liable to or deserving of punishment or condemnation because he or she is responsible for a wrong.

> **James 1:12-16**
>
> "Blessed is anyone who endures temptation. Such a one has stood the test and will receive the crown of life that the Lord has promised to those who love him. No one, when tempted, should say, 'I am being tempted by God'; for God cannot be tempted by evil and he himself tempts no one. But one is tempted by one's own desire, being lured and enticed by it; then, when that desire has conceived, it gives birth to sin, and that sin, when it is fully grown, gives birth to death. Do not be deceived, my beloved."

If you were completely free to kill or not to kill, and you knew exactly what your actions would bring about, you are likely to be guilty of first-degree murder. You intended your actions to result in someone's death, and you freely chose to kill. But when you ratchet down the levels of knowledge and freedom, you could be guilty of second-degree murder (unpremeditated killing), manslaughter in the first degree (unpremeditated killing provoked by the victim's words or actions), manslaughter in the second degree (accidental killing), or negligent homicide (death caused by gross negligence regarding the victim). In the case of negligent homicide, it may only have been the case that you left the gate open to your pool so that a child fell in and drowned. In this case, it is only your lack of action (an omission) that caused the death of someone else. Clearly, you are less responsible for that death than is someone who intentionally planned and caused a death.

Responsible Responders in Community

In the section above I observed that it is Jesus Christ who is the model for humanity. This is true for all Christians — in the past, in the present, and in the future. God has designed our lives so that we might be like God, and live in everlasting friendship with God. This relationship without end is what makes us who we are. The call to be godlike is also our task. And the fact that life everlasting is to be spent with God is our motive for preparing ourselves now. The first task of Christians is to answer Yes to the God who calls us into relationship, and into our vocations. By vocation I do not mean a paid job; I mean the calling all humans have to love God, one another, and creation. Recognizing that this relationship is the foundation of our life and our morality is crucial for us to build lives that are both well constructed and beautiful.

We also have a basic set of human relationships that determine who we are, and these relationships limit our freedoms and responsibilities. The first chapter of Genesis describes male and female as being created together: "male and female created he them." In the creation story that appears in the second chapter of Genesis, God says, "It is not good that man should be alone," and then creates woman as the ideal complement to man. In each narrative, God creates not a solitary being but a pair. To be a person requires that we become part of the human conversation. None of us speaks a language that is only her or his own language. Our speech derives meaning from words spoken or written before in that language. When we become a part of the human family, we participate in its conversation.

Our relationships define who we are. I, for example, have been chosen by God as a Christian. I, in turn, have chosen to be married, and my wife and I now have children. I am a white male of a specific height and weight and humor. I am no longer free to "un-choose" these things, and the fact that I have these relationships defines who I am. Nevertheless, within this web of relationships I am still free to make a wide range of moral choices. And it is within this web of relationships that I discover who I am.

Philosopher Charles Taylor illustrates the importance of knowing who we are in relationship to one another with this illustration:

> If I asked you where Mt. Tremblant is, and you blindfolded me, took me up in a plane, and then removed the blindfold when we were directly over Mt. Tremblant and said, "There, that's Mt. Tremblant," that would not help me know where the mountain is. We must know our place as we find it in relationship. (Taylor, 41)

Our relationships also determine our responsibilities. Some of these responsibilities we willingly assume, and others come to us without our willing them. For example, as a father I quite willingly take responsibility for my children. But if my wife were to die and I thus became a single parent, I would have to take on that added responsibility even though I had not chosen to do so. On the other side of the parent-child relationship is the fact that my children, who now receive my support, may one day need to care for me. Neither I nor they would likely desire to be in this situation, but given the depth of the relationship between parent and child, such a responsibility might ensue. To be in a relationship is to accept responsibility; to lose a relationship is to lose a piece of the self.

Each of us is someone in particular as soon as we are born. All humans are born into a specific context that makes them who they are — a poor Indian boy, a sickly but smart English girl, an athletic Indonesian boy, and so on. The Christian moral agent is unique because his or her foundational relationship is with Christ. This foundational relationship is the source of his/her identity. In addition, each Christian agent becomes part of the ongoing body of Christ — the church. The characteristic that gives someone a specifically Christian identity is not based on gender, race, nation, income — not on any of the things we typically use to define ourselves and others. Christian identity is based on a relationship to the life and work of Jesus Christ and his church. We become part of Christ's church if we are baptized into it. By saying that we are Christians, we become a part of this long line of sinful saints of Christ's church, and our identity is shaped by it.

Finally, we are created in relationship with the living world. We are physical beings who are part of the eco-community that includes all beings on our planet. We were created in relationship to all of them — donkeys and dogs, parakeets and pythons, red maples and red-winged blackbirds. The responsibility we have for them is great, for we are God's appointed caretakers of the world. We are made up of its chemicals, and we breathe and breed the same way that other mammals do. When we act, it is our bodies that do the acting. And we often act out of a direct response to what our body senses — hunger, thirst, fatigue, anxiety, pain, and so forth.

Cyberspace Ethics

Are you part of a community with someone you know only in cyberspace?

Does being in community with someone require close physical contact with him?

What might you lose if you are not physically close to him?

Although ethics is often seen as a way of making decisions, it occurs within a physical context in which we respond to our environment. Richard Niebuhr reminds Christians that it is God who acts within creation, and thus his recommendation for moral action is this: "God is acting in all actions upon you. So respond to all actions upon you as you respond to [God's] action" (Niebuhr, p. 126). In this way Niebuhr reminds us that God is guiding the history of the world, and even its physical events, so that when we respond to them, we are responding to God's actions. This leads to a dynamic ethic in which we as moral agents are constantly in dialogue with God via God's acts in the world.

Ending Questions

1. We sometimes let someone else take responsibility for us when we shouldn't, or refuse to give someone else responsibility when we should. Can you think of any examples when responsibility is wrongly placed?

2. How much responsibility do you have, or do you feel you have, for evils that occur in other countries?
3. Can you give examples of times when you were held responsible for something, but in fact you were not? How about vice versa?
4. Is the physical still seen as dirty among some Christians?
5. In what ways might passion be an impediment to responsibility, and in what ways a stimulant for responsibility?
6. How is the Christian sense of vocation different from a job or profession?

Works Cited and Further Reading

Brown, W. S., H. Newton Malony, and Nancey Murphy, eds. *Whatever Happened to the Soul? Scientific and Theological Portraits of Human Nature.* Minneapolis: Fortress, 1998.

Green, Joel B. *Body, Soul and Human Life: The Nature of Humanity in the Bible.* Grand Rapids: Baker, 2008.

Gula, Richard M., S.S. *The Call to Holiness.* New York: Paulist Press, 2003.

Hamer, Dean. *The God Gene: How Faith Is Hardwired into Our Genes.* New York: Anchor Books, 2004.

Hoekema, Anthony. *Created in God's Image.* Grand Rapids: Eerdmans, 1986.

Jeeves, Malcolm, ed. *From Cells to Souls and Beyond: Changing Portraits of Human Nature.* Grand Rapids: Eerdmans, 2004.

Lewis, C. S. "The Weight of Glory." In *The Weight of Glory.* Grand Rapids: Eerdmans, 1966.

Middleton, J. Richard. *The Liberating Image: The Imago Dei in Genesis 1.* Grand Rapids: Baker, 2005.

Niebuhr, H. Richard. *The Responsible Self.* San Francisco: Harper and Row, 1963.

Peterson, James C. *Changing Human Nature: Ecology, Ethics, Genes, and God.* Grand Rapids: Eerdmans, 2010.

Taylor, Charles. *Sources of the Self.* Cambridge, MA: Harvard University Press, 1989.

CHAPTER FOUR

Sin

Of man's first disobedience, and the fruit
Of that forbidden tree whose mortal taste
Brought death into the world, and all our woe,
With loss of Eden, till one greater Man
Restore us, and regain the blissful seat,
Sing Heavenly Muse. . . .
Say first (for Heaven hides nothing from thy view,
Nor the deep tract of Hell), say first what cause
Moved our grand parents, in that happy state,
Favored of Heaven so highly, to fall off
From their Creator, and transgress his will
For one restraint, lords of the world besides?
Who first seduced them to that foul revolt?

*   The infernal serpent; he it was, whose guile,*
Stirred up with envy and revenge, deceived
The mother of mankind, what time his pride
Had cast him out from Heaven, with all his host
Of rebel angels, by whose aid, aspiring
To set himself in glory above his peers,
He trusted to have equaled the Most High,
If he opposed; and with ambitious aim
Against the throne and monarchy of God,
Raised impious war in Heaven and battle proud,
With vain attempt.

John Milton, *Paradise Lost*, Book One, 1-6, 27-44

Definitions

Sin is mysterious. Why? Why did our ancient parents choose the wrong? What folly caused the serpent to challenge the Almighty? Reflective people, including great poets like John Milton, have long asked these questions. In this chapter we will investigate sin, but I should warn you in advance that I will not answer the great questions that Milton asks. Nonetheless I do hope that we will gain some clarity on what sin and evil are.

What is sin? I don't ask you to name a specific sin, such as murder, theft, or adultery. Rather, what is sin itself? It's important to ask this question because it is the counterpoint to asking what is good, and right, and virtuous. When we engage in ethics, we study how to become virtuous, to do the right, and seek the good. This presumes that their opposites — vice, wrong, and evil — are real possibilities. In fact, Saint John describes Jesus' task in this way: "The Son of God appeared for the very purpose of undoing the devil's work" (1 John 3:8). In a sense, Christian ethics is a strategy for continuing Jesus' task of undoing the work of the devil. I will first set up some basic definitions of terms related to sin. Though these definitions bleed into each other, separating the terms should help us understand the subject.

The word "sin" (as a singular concept) can be thought of as a condition — for example, "We are born in sin." This means that all humans are naturally at odds with, and alienated from, God. As a result, we are also at odds with and alienated from other people, ourselves, plants, and animals. This is now the common state of affairs for all humans. We can't say, "Dear God, could you please make my part of the world one in which sin does not play a part?" By being born as humans in this world, we share in its sinfulness. The condition of sinfulness has sometimes been called "original sin," but that may not be the best way to describe it. Perhaps "universal" or "common" sin would be better. This understanding of "sin" gets at the notion that we are, right from the beginning and in our essence, not right with God or God's moral standards. Each of us — and all parts of each of us — are touched by the condition of sin into which we were born. And this will not change. Our children and grandchildren, people in China and Russia, astronauts and deep-sea divers — all have the same problem. It is inescapable.

It was once thought that sin — or the fall into sin — meant that we as humans lost one aspect of our human nature. For example, some early theologians believed that when Adam and Eve fell into sin, we humans retained the "image" of God but lost the "likeness." Others held that we lost "supernatural" virtues while retaining "natural" ones. But sin is not only the loss of the image of God, or of the human spirit, or any one aspect of our person. It is a problem in the whole nature of the whole person who, by virtue of being born as a human, is by nature turned away from God.

Some people today also seem to believe that when we sin, it is only one part of us that does so. For example, I'm told that there are some prostitutes in Latin America who keep statues of saints, especially one of Mary Magdalene, in their rooms. The implication seems to be that, while the prostitutes may sin with their bodies, in their hearts they are really good people. While I realize that most prostitutes are poor women who have been compelled by their economic situation to sell the only resource they have left, I cannot agree that their souls are pure while they sin with their bodies. We sin as whole persons. My left hand is me just as my brain is me. If I sin with either one, it is I who sin. If I sin in thought or word or deed, it is *my* thought or word or deed.

Sin is not the same as a physical limitation. For example, we are limited in what we can do because of the nature of our bodies, our geographical location, and so on. But the fact that a professional basketball player can jump much higher than you can does not make him a better person than you are; it only makes him a better jumper. The limitations you have in leaping ability and earning power are not sins that you should worry about. They are simply natural limitations that pertain to you. Neither my body nor yours is evil, even in their great limitations. Therefore, a suppression of "the flesh" is not an effective remedy for sin. When Saint Paul used the term "flesh," he had in mind the temporal and temptable nature that all humans have. "The flesh" was a characteristic way of referring to those who have not participated in the life of the Spirit. It refers more to an epoch in history than to the physical aspect of our selves. Real moral limitations are the result of being controlled by our own vices. A virtuous person is like a moral athlete who can perform a wide range of good.

"Sins" (plural), on the other hand, refer to particular actions that are wrong. If I cheat on a test, that is a particular sin. If I harm someone by using words to slander her, that, too, is a sin. Sins are specific. We don't sin in general; we do particular things that are really wrong. We often like to gloss over our sins with words like "mistakes" or "regrets." But most are really sins. A mistake is merely an error: for example, if we add up numbers incorrectly, such an error (or mistake) is not a moral event; it is an amoral one. A regret is something we feel after we sin (I'll discuss that further when we address *conscience*). Sins are actual and particular wrongs for which we are responsible. Nor is sin a sickness. To say "the serial killer is a very sick man" is not an accurate or complete description of the killer. Sickness implies something that is uncontrollable and unwanted in our bodies or minds. Saying that the serial killer is sick pretends that the willful sinner is no less culpable for his crimes than the sick person is for catching a virus.

Sin (singular): A condition in which humans stand in opposition to God and God's standard for morality

Sins (plural): Particular infractions or instances of wrongdoing, e.g., lying, stealing, coveting, killing

Concupiscence: The intractable desire humans have toward evil

Evil: Harmful intent and hurtful consequences

"Concupiscence" is probably not a word you hear very often, but it is useful in making distinctions about sin. Concupiscence is our unshakable desire for evil. This desire is at the root of all sins. We desire the wrong things, in the wrong ways, at the wrong times. The fact that we have this desire is the root of the problem. Concupiscence is the desire for evil, and its tale is first told in the third chapter of Genesis. Notice the story of the first sin: "The woman looked at the tree: the fruit would be good to eat; it was pleasing to the eye and desirable for the knowledge it could give" (Gen. 3:6). That does sound good, doesn't it? Sin is appealing, tasty, and desirable. We like what it will do for us, the experience we'll gain from it, the pleasure it will provide, and the fact that we will no longer be naïve about these kinds of things. This is the trick of the evil one. He takes something that is good and puts it to evil use. "Look how good it is, child of Eve, you can't pass that up!" Like our parents Adam and Eve, we want to redefine good and evil. We tell ourselves a lie. We deceive ourselves into believing that what we are doing is really okay for us — at least for now. We think that illegal copying of music CDs, because it's possible, is okay to do, or sex outside of marriage is as good as it is within marriage, or good food or drink may be used to the point of gluttony or drunkenness.

Those sins deemed by the church over the centuries to be the "seven deadly" sins are really desires: pride, envy, anger, sloth, greed, gluttony, and lust. Notice that not one of them is an action; instead, they are all desires that lead to sin(s) and bring about its evil consequences. Envy, for example, might lead us to theft, or might make us neglect our family in order to make more money, or might turn our language bitter and vicious. Lust can result in illicit sex or perverse fantasies; it could also lead to evil conditions of mistrust, sexual dissatisfaction in marriage, or the denigration of other persons into sex toys. "Out of the heart are the issues of [humans]" is what the Bible says. And the positive biblical formulation against lust is: "Blessed are the pure in heart, for they shall see God."

Christian ethics also deals with the heart. How can we tune our hearts in such a way that they vibrate sympathetically with virtue and are out of tune with vice? Unfortunately, the answer is the same one that we tell anyone who wants to become an expert at something: practice, practice, practice.

The role of the imagination in the process of sin is important. We must first imagine what it would be like to do something wrong. We think of its pleasure; we delight in seeing ourselves as being worldly and sophisticated like other people who do it; we think that norms of behavior do not apply to someone as special as we are. But sin begins with one really big lie: we imagine that what is evil is really good.

The source of sin is self-delusion. We find that a certain kind of sin is appealing, and we tell ourselves that this is the kind of person we would like to be. But proper views of the self must be held up to the light of the person of Christ, who is the aim of our

Case Study

Is viewing porn really a sin? Sex was created by God, and it is good. So sex in itself is not sinful. And John is not married, so he is not cheating on someone. But it does seem to be an evil desire. He wants the bodies of those women on the screen. He sees them as pretty tasty temptations. But they aren't real, at least not in his dorm room; they're just up on his computer monitor. Would he have to actually go out and hire a prostitute to be considered sinning?

life. When we delude ourselves about who we are and who we ought to become, we also invite others to confirm our delusion. Good (positive) people become those who confirm us in our pleasant but false self-delusions, and bad (negative) people are the ones who challenge our view of ourselves. But the opposite is true: the heart of sin is lying to the self. We tell ourselves that we are something other than what we ought to be. We deny our source and our destiny in Christ. We are called away to false selves. But those who challenge our self-delusions in the light of Christ's knowledge call us to our true destiny. This is the task of church.

Is it sinful to sidestep solutions to evil in the world?

It seems that many Christians shove the question of evil off to the side once they have addressed the issue of salvation. That is, once they tell others that their sins must be forgiven, they feel that their duty is done. Or once they acknowledge that apartheid and slavery were evil, the subject is closed. But God's justice requires that the very human conditions of injustice and evil be ameliorated or eradicated.

The term "evil" refers more to the consequences of sin than to a specific act, and thus we might define "evil" as harm done or intended. That is, people can be said to be "evildoers" when they are plotting and doing harm. Some people do great evil; others do little evil and much good. So evil, unlike sin, is not a condition that all share in equally. It can happen that the same sin produces far greater evil in one instance than another. For example, I might tell my spouse a lie to cover my tracks, and she may later catch me in my lie, which could produce harmful results for both of us. But if a politician tells a similar lie to cover his tracks, he could produce an enormous amount of evil. My sin might have destructive consequences for my marriage, but the same sin of the politician might bring evil and tragic consequences to an entire nation.

Great evil is often a reaction to an initial lesser evil, and thus it may serve as a judgment on that previous evil. The prophet Hosea says, "They sow the wind and reap the whirlwind" (Hosea 8:7), and in saying this he is warning that those who do some small evil may well be repaid with enormous evil. The Christian response to evil is not exactly the same as its response to sin. Sin merits repentance: "Oh Lord, forgive me, for I have sinned." Evil is not as clear as sin, nor is repentance its solution. Evil may have developed over a great length of time, so that it may be infused into political or economic or family systems.

Christians need not so much to repent, but to turn from evil and seek to rectify it. To remove the evil, we need to change the harmful conditions that cause it. For example, an evil condition such as apartheid or slavery must be removed, and the violence and fear that resulted for black South Africans and African-Americans must be replaced by peace, justice, and hope. The worst of evils — and the greatest harm — have been removed by Christ: in so doing he brought about the greatest possible good. Thus what Paul tells us in Romans is now possible: "Do not repay evil for evil," and "Do not be overcome by evil, but overcome evil with good" (Rom. 12:17, 21).

To summarize, we have made basic distinctions among the terms: sin is a condition of opposition to God; sins are particular wrongful actions; concupiscence is a desire for evil; and evil refers to the destructive human consequences of our wrong actions.

Salvation enters in at all points. Salvation removes the problem of sin as the condition that alienates us from God. Then the presence of Christ's Spirit gives us resources to overcome individual sins. Concupiscence is reduced, and our desire to do evil is lessened. Through God's grace and our work, we overcome evil and its effects. We become actors not only in the history of sin but also in the work of salvation in Christ.

Next I will try to answer the question of what sin is by turning to biblical metaphors. The Bible provides many descriptions — sometimes graphic ones — of sin.

Sin in Literature

Novelists are often much better at describing sin and evil than theologians are. For example, William Golding wrote *Lord of the Flies* about British boys who were stranded on an island, far from sinful society. It turns out in the plot of his novel, however, that sin was quite near and will affect all of them.

Graham Greene also explored the ugly contours of sin in a number of his novels, including *The Comedians* and *The Power and the Glory.*

Biblical Metaphors for Sin

The first metaphors I'll mention have to do with location or placement: trespassing, straying, coming short, and missing the mark. Notice that all of these assume a path or target. There is a norm, and sin misses that norm. Right conduct is like the bull's-eye: an immoral action is off target and is a sin. Another metaphor is that of distance. We should arrive at point D, but we only get to point C. This "falling short" is also a picture of sin. A third metaphor for sin is that of the right route or path. The norm for moral action is like following highway signs that direct us to go northeast; sin heads west on a gravel road instead. This "straying," or "leaving the straight and narrow path," is a depiction of sin. Yet another boundary metaphor is that of trespassing. When we are clearly told "Keep Out!" we nevertheless tramp on in, and that is sin. Similarly, sin is what is twisted: what was once straight is now contorted. You can certainly think of things that you and others have done that might be described by these images of sin.

Another set of depictions for sin has to do with the composition of something. Let's say you have a glass of fresh, clean water. That is a picture of something that is good and pure. But if you take some oil and sludge from your garage and mix it in the water, it becomes impure and polluted. This is another metaphor for sin. What was once pure is now corrupt; what was clear and clean is now impure and spoiled. This picture has often been used concerning marital infidelity. A pure marriage relationship is between one man and one woman; an impure one occurs when another element is introduced, thus corrupting the marriage. A related picture of evil is that of chaos. In the beginning God called order out of chaos. A messy world was made orderly by establishing clear divisions between light and dark, water and land, earth and sky, and so on. Evil is sometimes pictured as the return of chaos or a breakdown of order such as in the story of the flood, in which uncontrolled waters destroy all living things on the earth.

Another set of metaphors has to do with the marketplace. When Jesus said, "Forgive us our debts, as we forgive our debtors," he presented a classic statement of this type. Sin means we are indebted to — and thus under the power of — a creditor. A debt of sin must be paid before we can go forward with our business. Related to this metaphor of debt is the picture of bondage. Sin binds us and we can't get out.

Sin can also be viewed as an assault on or offense to things that are as they should be: we forcefully change them to achieve our own devious goals. We slap the established order in the face. We assault the good that God has placed in the world, and in doing so we insult the God who put them there. Like Adam and Eve, we say, "No, I'd rather do it my way." We disobey. This implies the notion of turning against or betraying. We know who the real author of good and evil is, but we think that our way is better.

Finally, sin can be viewed as "disturbing the peace." Disturbing the peace is a misdemeanor in the United States. But in the Bible, disturbing the peace is much more severe. This is because peace, or *shalom,* is not merely a place that does not experience much noise or violence. Shalom is a picture of wholeness, health, and goodness. It is a condition in which relationships between God and humans, relationships among humans, and the relationships between humanity and creation are delightful. We are not at odds with anything or anyone; we don't have conflict. There is something of a cosmic sigh that says, "Yes, this is the way it should be." Sin breaks that peace.

However, there is a cure for this: it is salvation. When people ask for forgiveness and receive the new life of Christ, their status before God changes. To use the pictures of sin presented above, we are put on the right path, we are purified, our debts are paid, and we are released; we are acquitted of our crimes, and we are at peace. Nevertheless, until Christ returns, we fight the presence of sin and concupiscence within ourselves. We continue to commit various sins. These sins do not have the power to undo our salvation, but they do have the power to sidetrack us from the path of discipleship and make us less effective in God's service. While the *state* of sin is overthrown by the work of Christ, the work of *staying free* from sins and evil is a daily task.

In Ephesians 4:22-24, Paul says: "You were taught, with regard to your former way of life, to put off your old self, which is being corrupted by its deceitful desires; to be made new in the attitude of your minds; and to put on the new self, created to be like God in true righteousness and holiness." This is the Christian task. We were the perfect image of God, are now no longer, but one day will again be so. Reimaging God is our work and God's work in us. As Paul says elsewhere, "Therefore, my dear friends . . . continue to work out your salvation with fear and trembling, for it is God who works in you to will and to act according to his good purpose" (Phil. 2:12-13).

Sin's Effects

All sin is dehumanizing. It breaks down the persons that we could be and should be. It tears the fabric of our relationship with God, others, creation, and even within ourselves. As I have noted earlier, the relationship that we have with God is affected by the condition of sin: everything is wrong between us and God. Our relationship with God includes alienation, shame, guilt, and mistrust. The first result of the Fall into sin was an evasion of responsibility. "She did it." "The serpent made me do it." We do not want to own up to what we do, and we are most reluctant to admit our responsibility for sin. We realize that if we do admit responsibility for our sin, there will be a price to pay.

Sin also affects others. Sometimes its effects are direct and clear. If I steal your car, you are harmed by my action. But some sins are less direct in their effects. For example, if I steal your car, I might also hurt many people in your neighborhood who now believe that they need a security system to protect their properties. I have taken away their freedom to hold their property without fear. This is a situation characterized by more evil and fear than the one in which they lived before I stole the car.

The effects of sin can also carry over long periods of time. The sins of slavery in the United States and apartheid in South Africa have had long-term effects in each of those societies. Though it has been many generations since there were slaves in America, the evil effects of the denigration of black people lives on. Though apartheid is no longer the law in South Africa, the existence of poor and violent townships is a direct result of that policy. This seems to be the way that sin has always worked. Listen to the second commandment.

> You must not make a carved image for yourself, nor the likeness of anything in the heavens above, or on the earth below, or in the waters under the earth. You must not bow down to them in worship; for I, the LORD your God, am a jealous God, punishing the children for the sins of the parents to the third and fourth generation of those who reject me. (Exod. 20:4-5)

The effects of this sin apparently can last for three or four generations. Is this because God holds a grudge? I doubt whether that would be the right way to describe it. But God is quite serious about the effects of sin. They often stick to the sinner and the sinner's children. This ugly truth is often borne out in history. Social scientists have shown us that there are generational cycles of abuse. Children pay for their parents' sins either in their person or in their society. The child of gamblers may receive no inheritance. The child of an alcoholic is more likely to have health problems, suffer violence, and become an alcoholic than is the child of the nonalcoholic.

Sin also affects our relationship with creation. We abuse the world we have been divinely commissioned to protect and cultivate: "The LORD God took the man and put him in the Garden of Eden to work it and take care of it" (Gen. 2:15). But in the condition of sin, the earth resists us and makes our lives hard.

Yet we can be thankful that things are not as bad as they could be. Due to the grace of God poured out on all humanity (often called "common grace"), conditions can often be quite good. God restrains sin and its effects. This often comes about by means of human institutions such as government, marriage, or business. The government stops many crimes by establishing laws that promote the good. Marriage keeps two people together in what they hope will be a lifelong commitment to the good of the other. Businesses provide useful products and services. This is true not only for Christians but for all humans. This may be another way of saying that sin is not the whole story in human history. Common grace (a gift of God to all) enables people to avoid some sin and evil.

Sin and Salvation

Overcoming sin and reestablishing right relationships with God, others, self, and the creation is the main story line of Scripture. Augustine (354-430 CE) described the relationship that Christians have with sin in four phases. Graphically, it can be seen as in the table at the top of page 62.

Pre-Fall Humans	Post-Fall Humans	Reborn Humans	Glorified Humans
able to sin	able to sin	able to sin	able to not sin
able to not sin	unable to not sin	able to not sin	unable to sin

In the first phase, the human's original capacities included both the power to not sin and the power to sin. In the second phase, after Adam and Eve's sin, humans lost the power to not sin and retained the power to sin. In the third phase of the Christian life, we are able to sin, but we are also able to refrain from sin. In the fourth phase, which is the fulfillment of grace, glorified humans will have the ability to sin taken away and receive the highest of all, the power not to be able to sin (Augustine, *Enchiridion,* XXXI, para. 118). These are the conditions of sin and grace that relate to Christians.

Varieties of Sin?

While it is true that all people are sinners — that is, that we all live in the condition of sin — it is not true that all sinners and sins are equal. Some sins and sinners are far worse than others. It is far worse to kill someone than to tell someone a white lie. The Roman Catholic tradition devised a classification system in which some sins are said to be "mortal," and others "venial."

> *Mortal sin* destroys charity in the heart of man by a grave violation of God's law; it turns man away from God, who is his ultimate end and his beatitude, by preferring an inferior good to him. *Venial sin* allows charity to subsist, even though it offends and wounds it. (*Catechism of the Catholic Church,* 1855)

If I understand this distinction correctly, both mortal and venial sins are what I have defined as sin*s* (in the plural). Venial sins do not have an effect on saving/sanctifying grace, which delivers us from the condition of sin. However, mortal sins do have an effect on saving/sanctifying grace. They return sinners to the condition they were in before they received that grace.

Most Protestants would reject this distinction, arguing that all sin offends God, and grace removes any sin, no matter what it is or when it is committed. But in the context of the confessional booth, the Catholic distinction is useful. Graver sins require a greater sense of responsibility and repentance than lighter sins do. One sin can be worse than another at any point of the moral triad. The moral agent may have very bad intentions, or the norm may be one that is very significant (e.g., taking a life versus taking a bracelet), or the outcome may have widely harmful effects. So an act performed with great malicious intent and against an important norm — and having wide-ranging evil consequences — is far worse than an act performed with little malice, against a minor rule, with few evil results. The first act will place a greater obstacle between ourselves and God — or neighbor, or creation, or self — than will a minor infraction. Thus, while the distinction between mortal and venial sins may be somewhat arbitrary, the desire to show that some sins are graver than others and cause a greater obstacle to a life of discipleship is a helpful tool.

While sins can be grave and profound or smaller (e.g., "white lies") and less significant, other actions that aren't good may not even be called sin. We call many such actions or attitudes "folly." For example, not changing the oil in your car or not studying for a test can be foolish, but they are not sins. You didn't act in opposition to a moral norm, have malicious intent, or cause evil; nevertheless, they were foolish things to do. Folly is often contrasted to wisdom in the Bible. Wisdom sees how the world goes and should go — and acts accordingly. Folly either does not see or does not care about how the world goes, and acts carelessly. Folly also has goals that are not worthy of a human being with a divine destiny. For example, you may have become the best Game-Boy player on your block. Congratulations! You have achieved a great height of folly.

Some folly, though, is also sin. For example, getting sexually involved with another person who is not your spouse is foolish, and it is also a sin. Such an act requires repentance. A foolish act might have negative consequences, but it is not the kind of thing that demands repentance. I don't need to repent for not changing my car's oil. Sinful actions do require repentance, but foolish actions don't. Sometimes the proper response to folly may be a good chuckle.

Some sins are also crimes, and some are not. For example, it is a sin to dishonor your parents by yelling obscenities at them, but it is not a crime. It would, however, become a crime if you hit and intentionally injured one of them or stole from them. There are two reasons why some sins may not be crimes. First, you may sin in your thoughts but not in your deeds. You could, for example, despise someone in your heart, which is a sin ("Never seek revenge or cherish a grudge towards your brother; you must love your neighbor as yourself" [Lev. 19:18]).

Gambling

How about gambling? Is it folly? Or is it sin?

Are there circumstances when it could be folly but not sin?

Yet, even though this attitude is a sin, the civil authorities cannot and will not charge you with a crime, because you have not performed any action that requires the attention of government authorities.

The second reason that some sins are not crimes is that their object — the one sinned against — is not the object that the civil authorities are commissioned to protect. In simpler language, you can sin against God and not commit a crime. You might take up God's name in vain and imaginative ways; you might construct idols that take over your life; or you might regularly profane the Sabbath day. But none of these will get you in trouble with the police. They shouldn't. Since the seventeenth century, Western societies have distinguished between civil and religious laws. The government is in charge of enforcing civil law, and the church is in charge of the religious ones. (In some Islamic societies these two kinds of laws are not distinguished, and Islamic law, *sharia,* is also the law of civil society.)

Sin and crime are not understood in the same way in every culture. For example, in some cultures polygamy is not considered a sin; but in the cultures of most of the developed societies today, it is considered against the law. One sin may be seen as more grave in one culture than another as well. For example, showing disrespect to a parent or grandparent in China is thought of as a far greater evil than it would be in most homes in the United States. It also seems to be true that some sins are more prevalent in one culture than another.

In summary, this chapter has spoken quite a bit about sin. But be aware that knowing that something is sinful does not inoculate you against it. If that were the case, ethicists would be the world's best people! And education would be the cure for sin. In reality, you and I may know very well that action X is sinful — and nevertheless go right ahead with it. Or we may delude ourselves into believing that this time this sin is okay. We do this because of concupiscence, or as Paul puts it, the "old nature" that we still have. While we may be saved from sin, we are still weak, frail, and temptable. This is why Jesus does not instruct us to go to school and read up on morality when we are attracted to evil; instead, he instructs us to ask God to "lead us not into temptation, but deliver us from evil."

Ending Questions

1. Is there a clear line between sin and folly? For example, if I fail to change the oil in my car to the degree that the engine seizes up and is destroyed, have I sinned by not taking care of a possession that God gave me?
2. Society generally views violent crime as worse than nonviolent crime. Is this right — even if nonviolent crimes may bring about greater evil?
3. Are sins of thought less significant than those of deeds?
4. How much is it the church's job to point out the sins of its members?
5. Is it right that some sins are not crimes?

Works Cited and Further Reading

Augustine, *Enchiridion.*
Bavinck, Herman. *Reformed Dogmatics,* vol. 3: *Sin and Salvation in Christ,* edited by John Bolt. Grand Rapids: Baker Academic, 2006.

Lewis, C. S. *The Screwtape Letters*. San Francisco: HarperSanFrancisco, 2001.

Midgley, Mary. *Wickedness: A Philosophical Essay*. Boston: Routledge and Kegan Paul, 1984.

Peck, M. Scott. *People of the Lie: The Hope for Healing Human Evil*. New York: Simon and Schuster, 1983.

Plantinga, Cornelius. *Not the Way It's Supposed to Be: A Breviary of Sin*. Grand Rapids: Eerdmans, 1996.

Simon, Caroline. *The Disciplined Heart: Love, Destiny, and Imagination*. Grand Rapids: Eerdmans, 1997.

Smedes, Lewis. *A Pretty Good Person*. San Francisco: Harper and Row, 1990.

Taylor, James. *Sin: A New Understanding of Virtue and Vice*. Winfield, BC: Northstone Publishing, 1997.

Verhey, Allen. "Evil." In *The International Standard Bible Encyclopedia,* edited by Geoffrey Bromiley. Grand Rapids: Eerdmans, 1982.

CHAPTER FIVE

Virtue

WHOM DO YOU like better, Cinderella or her stepmother? I'll put my money on Cinderella. Cinderella is the kind of good person we like, and the stepmother is the kind of evil person we don't like. Cinderella is virtuous, and her stepmother is vicious. Virtue is appealing; vice is repelling.

Both Cinderella and her stepmother seem to be capable and bright people. But Cinderella has virtues such as kindness and care, whereas her stepmother has vices such as envy, spitefulness, and greed. While people may have similar characteristics or personality traits, they may have very different vices and virtues. For example, being smart or strong does not, in itself, guarantee that you will be good. You could be a smart and strong thief, or you could use your strength and intelligence to become a skilled carpenter who builds homes for the poor. Being intelligent and having strength are abilities. When abilities such as these are aimed at a good, they can become virtues, and when aimed at evil, they can become vices.

Virtues aim at something. For example, if you are an acorn, your aim is to become an oak tree. Since you are a human, your life will aim at something as well. So what is it that humans aim toward? Can that be defined for everyone, or only for some people in particular communities? This has been a classical discussion in philosophy. What is the good life? After we answer that question, we can go on to ask which virtues will support us in our pursuit of that life.

To be a moral virtue, the good that you aim at must be a moral good. For example, I have the custom of carrying a wallet. I habitually arrange the bills in the wallet from (relatively) large to small, from back to front. But this habit is not a moral one; it is amoral. Wisdom is a virtue; arranging paper money in my wallet is not. For me to be virtuous, I would have to use that money wisely. A virtue is a habit that is aimed at a moral good, and when we speak of virtue, the issue is not so much what we should *do,* but who we should *become.* Becoming virtuous is a process that involves the mind, the emotions, the body, and the community.

A Brief History of Virtue

The subject of virtue is an ancient one. The Greeks and the Romans debated about which virtues were most important. For Plato (428-348 BCE), virtue is the knowledge of an ideal good, and vice is ignorance of that ideal. For Aristotle (384-322 BCE), virtues are part of practical wisdom that enables us to function well: reason must govern our passions so that we can achieve virtue. The Roman philosopher Cicero (106-43 BCE) is credited with first categorizing four virtues as "cardinal," which is a way of saying that these virtues are of the first order of importance. Cicero's cardinal virtues are courage, temperance, justice, wisdom. They regulate other virtues.

- Courage: How much should I allow fear to shape my actions?
- Temperance: How much should I satisfy my appetites?
- Justice: How do I give everyone his/her rightful due?
- Wisdom: What is the best course of action, all things considered?

Philosopher Jean Porter describes the roles of the cardinal virtues in this way: "Prudence or practical wisdom . . . enables the agent to choose in accordance with her overall conception of goodness; justice orients the will towards the common good; courage shapes the irascible passions in such a way as to resist obstacles to attaining what is truly good; and temperance shapes the passions of desire in such a way that the agent desires what is truly in accordance with the overall good" (Porter, 103).

Saint Augustine believed that the font of all true virtue is Christian love. The crucial point for him is that we place our loves in the proper order: first, the love for God, then love for the neighbor, and then love for created things. For Augustine, vice is a love that is wrongly ordered. For Saint Thomas Aquinas (1225-1274), there are two kinds of virtues: those that seek human goods and are regulated by reason (natural), and those that are given by God and seek union with him (spiritual). To the four cardinal virtues of antiquity, the Christian faith has added three that are unique to it: faith, hope, and love. Notice that these virtues articulated by Saint Paul are directed at the Christian's final moral good — God. Faith is in God, hope is in God, and love is for God. Tying virtue to Christian faith, Jean Porter says, "Virtues are the means by which grace becomes active" (Porter, 106).

Habit: a settled custom, practice, or usage

Custom: a habitual or usual practice

Character: a set of acquired and stable abilities and traits

Virtue: a habitual and practiced disposition toward a moral good

Vice: a habitual and practiced disposition toward a moral evil

The New Testament borrows those virtues from the Greco-Roman culture into which it was born. For example, Saint Paul calls on the Christians in Colossae to put off the vices that were common to that society and to put on the virtues common to it (Col. 3:5-13). He then says that his readers must add specifically Christian virtues to complete their character.

> Finally, to bind everything together and complete the whole, there must be love. Let Christ's peace be arbiter in your decisions, the peace to which you were called as members of a single body. Always be thankful. Let the gospel of Christ dwell among you in all its richness; teach and instruct one another with all the wisdom it gives you. (Col. 3:14-16)

When we speak of virtue, then, we are not addressing something that is foreign to non-Christians. We are speaking of something that is common to humans but uniquely shaped and directed by Christian faith. Christian virtues can direct and correct the other virtues. Each cardinal virtue could become something that we use for our own sake, were it not for the presence of Christian virtues that direct them toward God. For example, you might develop the virtue of courage because you would be admired for it, or you would feel good about it. But the virtues of faith, hope, and love would direct your courage in service to God and neighbor. Such courage would not be an achievement you could boast about; rather, it would be a tool that could be used in the service of God and his kingdom.

The Christian virtues are as much gift as they are achievement. Christian virtues are those we develop due to grace. We participate in the character traits of God. God cultivates Christian virtue within us, so it is as much God's work as ours. We receive the love of God, grow in hope in God, and increase our faith in God as he leads us and shows himself to be loving, faithful, and trustworthy. Other virtues develop as the result of our own practice. The theological virtues also require practice, but the virtues practice what God has given. The life and virtue of Jesus is the Christian standard for virtue. His practice of these virtues was perfect, as was his use of them in service to the Father and to his disciples.

Virtue and Vice

Aristotle showed that a virtue is an ideal mean; that is, it is not too much or too little. For example, note how the following virtues have vices on either side.

Deficiency	Mean	Excess
Cowardice	Courage	Recklessness
Impassiveness	Temperance	Intemperateness
Stinginess	Generosity	Extravagance
Sloppiness	Neatness	Meticulousness

You would love to have someone at your side who had these and other virtues, and you would be cherished if you were the person who was so virtuous. Virtues such as these encourage human thriving. They are what make a life good. If we were all courageous, temperate, just, and prudent, we would not need police. We would live long and happy lives. Virtues can sustain us in our quest for the good, or at least for our own good. But virtue is difficult: it requires that we be strict with ourselves, veering neither toward excess nor deficiency.

But we aren't necessarily strict with ourselves. That's because we are likely to be as full of vice as we are of virtue. A vice is the opposite of a virtue: it is a habitual and practiced disposition toward a moral evil. Vices must live off virtues because they cannot exist on their own. For example, fidelity in marriage is a virtue; infidelity is a vice in that it is the corruption of the virtue of fidelity. You must first be in a relationship of faithfulness before you can become unfaithful. The vice could not exist if there weren't already a virtue there for it to corrupt. And the movement from virtue to vice is often in small, subtle steps. For instance, you might just flirt a little with someone who is not your spouse, and then get together for a drink, and then find yourself in bed with that person without ever having made a conscious decision to commit adultery. At that final point it is clear enough that you have sinned, but before then it is difficult to pinpoint where sin occurred. You might argue that flirting and drinking are not sins in themselves, and you would probably be right. Nevertheless, some of our practices undermine virtue and lead to sin.

Case Study

Are Jerry and Lori being extravagant if they buy the condo? Being self-indulgent may be a vice, but it is not the worst of vices. And enjoying the good world that God has given us sounds to them like they would be developing the virtue of gratitude. If they decide to buy it — and at the same time resolve to be constantly grateful for it — would that work?

Some virtues — such as joy, gratitude, peace — are more emotional than others, such as temperance or prudence. Emotions come about as a result of the way we perceive things. For example, if a dog is running toward me, I will be happy if I see that it is my dog. However, if a neighborhood child sees my dog running toward her, she might become fearful. Those things that we have a hunger for or concern about are the ones that can touch our emotions. I care for my dog, so I don't want to see her attacked by another dog or left out in the cold too long. I am not just concerned for dogs in general, but specifically for my dog.

The way we construe what is happening largely determines the emotions we have about it. For example, in the story related in Acts 5:41, the disciples are beaten and then thrown into prison. For nearly everyone, beating and imprisonment would generate anger, sorrow, resentment, or humiliation. Yet in this case the disciples rejoice! This is because they interpret their suffering in light of their relationship to Christ. For them the beating and jailing is a mark of honor: they were counted as worthy of serving their Lord.

Not everything is worthy of passionate commitment. We can be passionate about the wrong things, or about trivial things. For example, I might take my favorite baseball team's loss so seriously that I become clinically depressed and can no longer function at home or at work. In this case, my dedication to the team is not a virtue, since the team is not an object that is worth that degree of dedication and emotional expense. Sometimes long-lasting passions can determine our character traits. For example, if I have a lifelong passion for the Chicago White Sox, I am a fan(atic) who is identified by my passion for that team and that game.

The Christian believes that she has an advantage in overcoming vice and cultivating virtue: the power of God via the Holy Spirit. The power of the Holy Spirit within the believer enables her to accomplish what she could not on her own. This is, in other words, part of the process of sanctification. Having been justified by faith, we seek to live life for God, and become like God in Christ. This belief presumes that the power of God is within us and enables us to pursue a godly life. For example, Alcoholics Anonymous has a twelve-step program to overcome addiction to alcohol. The first three steps are as follows:

1. We admit that we are powerless over alcohol — that our lives have become unmanageable.
2. We believe that a Power greater than ourselves could restore us to sanity.
3. We make a decision to turn our will and our lives over to the care of God (as we understand Him).

Vice can take over our lives. We can become the slave of the vice rather than its master. Alcoholics Anonymous and other twelve-step groups recognize this. They know that we must find something outside of and greater than ourselves in order to overcome vice.

Vice is not necessarily something that is intrinsically evil; it can be a lesser good that has taken the place of a greater good. For example, I do not believe that alcohol is bad in itself, but when it becomes the thing that we seek obsessively above friends, family, or God, it has usurped their places. Nice clothing is not evil either. But when we shop for clothes in order to make ourselves feel important or to stave off depression, it may be taking over a role it should not have — and thus it becomes a vice. In a way, the moral life of a Christian disciple may be seen as the progression from vice to virtue. In order for this to happen, there are some basic steps that everyone follows.

a. We resist vice and draw away from it.
b. We begin to practice its corresponding virtue (which may entail a swing toward the other extreme).
c. We become constant in our practice of virtue.

Becoming virtuous is a process, not an event. But we can be thankful that growing in virtue can progress even when physical strength diminishes. Virtues are both an inclination and a skill. It is not enough to say that we have the inclination to be generous when we do not in fact give generously. The inclination is the motivation, and the skill is the ability. Both can be developed. I may increase my motivation toward generosity by acquainting myself with the poor and their needs. I can then become skillful in the giving of my time and resources to practice this virtue.

There is no guarantee that virtue increases with age. In fact, we might pick up more vices as we grow older. Like the ability to play a musical instrument, virtue can decay over time without practice. When I was first learning to play the piano, I had to practice scales. I played scales in every key; I played them with different rhythms; I played them in contrary motion as well as hands together. It was dull and tiresome work, but as I learned the scales, I gained the ability to play a lot of other music. My skill in scales made playing concert pieces or jazz far easier. Though I never became a virtuoso, I can still enjoy my capacity to make music at the piano. My practiced skill continues to give me freedom and joy, as does any virtue when we practice it. We gain the freedom to perform at high levels of moral sensitivity and competence. But if we don't practice virtue, we'll never perform it.

It is possible for a virtue to be used in service of evil. For example, members of the Mafia are said to be characterized by a very high level of loyalty and devotion. Yet the Mafia is devoted to doing evil. It may well be that there is "honor among thieves," that burglars may have a great deal of patience and courage, and that demons can also be courageous and prudent. But there can be no virtue in wrongdoing. For example, there is no such thing as a virtuous rape. This is why the Christian virtues have God as their ultimate end. The virtuous Christian enfolds his/her virtue in service of God and neighbor.

Case Study

Is John developing a vice when he watches porn? Lust? Intemperance? If so, what virtue is being diminished? Will this mean that he will have a harder time relating to his future wife sexually? Does he relate differently to women now than he should?

The trick to creating virtuous people is not merely to convince someone that virtue is a good thing. We might all quickly agree that it would be better for people to be generous, truthful, and courageous than stingy, deceitful, and scared. The trick in the development of virtue is to create a real desire for it, and then to put it into practice. For example, I might be able to convince you that the music of Stravinsky is better than that of Casting Crowns; but even so, you still might play Casting Crowns on your IPod instead of Stravinsky — simply because you like it better. Virtues, of course, are not the same as taste in music, but sometimes they can be treated that way. Virtues really are better than vices, but putting them into practice requires that we develop a taste for them. We must orient ourselves toward and prefer the virtuous. Then we must practice, practice, and practice to become virtuosos of virtue.

The practice of virtue can occur in a number of ways. Perhaps we can model a virtue, or we can "try it on," so to speak. We can practice it in different ways, like the musical scales I mentioned earlier. We can listen to tales of virtue in sermons, or see it enacted in liturgy or theater. We can spend time with people who possess the virtue we wish to have.

Different occupations typically require different character and virtue sets. For example, you would not expect a drill sergeant to have the same character and virtues that a social worker has. And that's fine. We are not all designed for the same vocation, and only together do Christians reflect the colors of the entire palette of Christian virtue. We tend to select our vocations in keeping with our character, and then to develop the virtues that are appropriate to that vocation.

A virtue is not a virtue until it is stable. For example, I'm not allowed to claim that I'm courageous if I protect my brother from the neighborhood bully every fourth time we pass through the neighborhood. Until a virtue is engrained into our character, we cannot claim it as our own.

Spanish Saying

The Spanish have a pithy saying about what we learn from our friends: "El que anda con lobos, aprende ladrar."

It means: "If you hang around with wolves, you'll learn to howl."

What virtues and vices characterize your group of friends?

Virtue and Culture

Do you think that some groups of people possess particular virtues and vices? I tend to. For example, while living in Latin America, I noticed that everyone seemed to practice the virtue of respect: "Si señor, para servirle, como usted gusta." (Yes sir, at your service, as you wish.) But after being there for some time, I came to understand that this virtue hid a vice: falsehood. While showing a great deal of the virtue of respect, people could allow the vice of falsehood to flourish. People in Latin America would not want to say something disrespectful to me, so they simply didn't tell me a great many things. To get at the truth of a matter often required considerable digging.

While in Japan, I learned that the Japanese think of North Americans as cowboys. We are seen by them as a bunch of loud, violent gunslingers. They are astonished that one can buy a gun in nearly any town in the United States. However, the seeming politeness of the Japanese may mask their own deception and perhaps violence. Their conquest of China and other Asian countries in the twentieth century was especially brutal. How can one explain this? Might it be that just as families have certain characteristic traits, so do cultures?

Within each culture honor is shown to those who possess that culture's virtues. For example, in the United States we honor business-people who build corporations and create jobs. We honor the beauty or skill of movie actors. On the other hand, those who reflect the vices of their culture are considered shameful. When a fat person fails to lose weight, or an athlete makes an error on a crucial play, he or she feels shame. Notice how culturally connected these ideas of honor and shame are. In some countries being heavy might mean that you are prosperous, and there are certainly cultures where few if any sports are very important. So you would be honored for being heavy, and no one would care if you could catch or kick a ball.

Jesus is a good counterweight to cultural virtues and vices. Jesus was not only a virtuous first-century Palestinian; he was a model of human virtue across cultures. As Douglas Ottati says, Jesus is a "concrete universal." Jesus actually lived as the perfect moral example and model. And the virtues that he practiced were put to service in the kingdom of God. When you read of the virtues mentioned in the Beatitudes, such as peacemaking and humility, you will find that they are practiced in the service of the kingdom of God, and they are in fact characteristics of the King's servants.

Stories of the virtuous are valuable, especially if the story is about someone you can relate to. For example, my grandmother was a poor immigrant who worked and served her family, her neighbors, her church, and her country. She had little education, but she taught me a thing or two when we played Scrabble. She was in many ways a model of virtue. Aiming my life in the direction in which she led hers is good. It might make my life virtuous, as was hers.

The church is God's school of character. Christians construe their lives in relationship to Jesus and respond to events that happen to them in the light of the way Jesus lived. In other words, we — the disciples — follow our rabbi and Lord, and the church carries on this tradition of discipleship. We tell each other the stories of people of faith who followed God in difficult times, and on rugged paths. We present these people as models of virtue for us to emulate today. And thus we model the Christian virtues.

Ending Questions

1. What are some things that are not evil in themselves that can become vices?
2. Are emotional virtues better than rational ones?
3. Why don't people necessarily become more virtuous with age?
4. Are some virtues easier to practice than others?
5. If you have lived in another culture, did you find virtues and vices that seemed to be characteristic of that culture?

Works Cited and Further Reading

Aristotle. *Nicomachean Ethics.* Translated by Terrence Irwin. Indianapolis: Hackett Publishing Co., 1985.

DeYoung, Rebecca Konyndyk. *Glittering Vices: A New Look at the Seven Deadly Sins and Their Remedies.* Grand Rapids: Brazos Press, 2009.

O'Connell, Timothy E. *Making Disciples: A Handbook of Christian Moral Formation.* New York: Crossroad/Herder, 1998.

Ottati, Douglas. *Jesus Christ and Christian Vision.* Louisville: Westminster John Knox Press, 1996.

Porter, Jean. "Virtue Ethics." In *The Cambridge Companion to Christian Ethics.* Cambridge, UK: Cambridge University Press, 2001.

Roberts, Robert C. *Spiritual Emotions: A Psychology of Christian Virtues.* Grand Rapids: Eerdmans, 2007.

Von Wright, G. H. *The Varieties of Goodness.* London: Routledge, 1963.

PART THREE

Norms

CHAPTER SIX

The Conscience

Of all the differences between man and the lower animals, the moral sense or conscience is by far the most important. . . . It is summed up in that short but imperious word "ought," so full of high significance. It is the most noble of all the attributes of man, leading him without a moment's hesitation to risk his life for that of a fellow-creature; or after due deliberation, impelled simply by the deep feeling of right or duty, to sacrifice it in some great cause.

Charles Darwin (cited in the prologue to Marc D. Hauser, *Moral Minds*)

All humans have a conscience. As Darwin observed, it is what makes us distinct from other creatures. The conscience is a very specific lens: its only focus is our own moral behavior. It is not a judge of beauty or truth, or strength or efficiency, or anything else. It is the judge of right and wrong that lives within us. It constantly asks, Was that good? Was that right? What if I did this? We hear these questions from our conscience, and we are wise to take them seriously.

This touch of conscience and the uneasy feeling it sometimes generates is the font of moral reflection. We sense that something is not quite right, and our very person is torn. This is the source of anxiety or dis-ease. The conscience is calling our attention to the fact that we do not meet up to our own standard or that we are becoming unhealthy.

The lack of integrity that our conscience announces calls out to our minds and souls for resolution. So we examine the conscience.

Theologian Timothy O'Connell notes that the conscience is a capacity, a process, and a judgment. Humans have the capacity to be morally self-directed: we go through a process of self-evaluation, and we make concrete judgments about things that we do or will do (O'Connell, p. 26). To have only one of these would not be enough. If we have the conscience as a capacity but do not engage it in a process of reflection, it is of little use. It would also be of little use if we were constantly reflecting but never arriving at a well-formed judgment. Our conscience speaks only to us; it does not address others. We might look at something that another person has done or said and think to ourselves, "I couldn't sleep at night if I pulled a stunt like that." But that is our moral judgment of someone else's action. That person's own conscience will have to convict him of the need for reflection or repentance. In this chapter I will ask and answer four questions about the conscience:

- Where do we get our conscience from?
- When does the conscience address us?
- Is the conscience always right?
- What makes the Christian conscience unique?

Where Do We Get Our Conscience From?

Recently, a number of scientists have attempted to explain the universal presence of the human conscience on the basis of human genetics. They propose that all humans have the innate genetic capacity to be moral. They use a technological analogy appropriate to our time: humans are like computers whose hardware is set up to handle morality, and our cultural influences are the specific moral programs on that hardware. Another analogy they use is one of language acquisition: all healthy babies can learn a language, but the particular language they learn depends on which one is spoken around them. These analogies present the conscience both as a capacity that is within us and as content that we get from outside ourselves.

Likening conscience to language may be particularly instructive. All humans communicate via language. Everyone must use the same common forms of communication, and the mental structure that enables all people to learn language is the same. For example, I could not communicate using only nouns, or by repeating the same musical note. I must form a sense unit (sentence) in a pattern that will be recognizable to others. All languages can be used to communicate if they follow normal linguistic patterns. So the Mandarin, English, and Hausa languages are all capable of carrying meaning, even though a speaker of one language may not understand people speaking the other two languages. I do not have to be a linguist or grammarian in any of these languages in order to speak intelligibly. I simply speak the language as I have heard it spoken. People who have learned a language constantly create new sentences, using grammatical rules of which they may not even be aware.

According to these studies, it seems that moral acquisition works in much the same way that language acquisition does. All humans are born with the capacity to develop morality. The specific content of our morality, however, is shaped by our context. If, for example, we are raised in a culture in which fathers execute daughters who become pregnant before being married, that moral standard is likely to be upheld by fathers in that culture. Though you and I may well agree that death is a terribly extravagant punishment for premarital sex, we may share with that culture the belief that morality does touch on our sexual practices. Therefore, though we might abhor the punishment structure of another culture, we might respond negatively to other sexual practices, be they promiscuity, homosexuality, or masturbation. While we may differ on the rightness or wrongness of any or all of these particular issues, we seem to be hard-wired in our belief that there are moral rights and wrongs about sexual practice.

As we speak about the development of the conscience, do not overlook the role of emotions. Recent brain research shows that an initial confrontation with a moral issue generates a high level of activity in the emotion-related areas of the brain (the prefrontal cortex). In the second place, we bring in the intellectual circuitry to do analysis. Lack of emotional connection is a terrible flaw in the formation of conscience. The conscience begins with — and requires — emotional connectedness. Being unconnected emotionally is the problem that a psychopath has. He may agree that torture is wrong, but he still may have no emotional restraints that actually prevent him from torturing.

(This view of the conscience as emotionally based contrasts with the more rationalistic approach of psychologist Lawrence Kohlberg, who proposed that higher levels of reasoning would produce higher levels of morality.)

The emotional bite of the conscience is not the same as a feeling of disgust. A feeling of disgust may indeed lead to the sense that something is morally wrong, but things that are disgusting are not necessarily immoral. For instance, you might be disgusted if a friend told you that he ate his lunch in a MacDonald's bathroom. Although disgusting, there is nothing immoral about that action. However, if that person told you that he had committed incest, your initial disgust would properly shift into moral outrage. In the first case, our quick emotional response of disgust stays at that level; in the second case, we add a judgment about the morality of the action to our initial feeling of disgust.

All humans, then, have feelings of disgust. We also all have a sense of right and wrong. Is the programming or the content of morality, then, related to God or God's law? Saint Paul indicates that it is. Romans 1:19-20 and 2:14-15 are two passages that express how all people have a conscience, not just the Jews who have the written law, or the Christians in Rome, whom Paul was addressing.

Church Teaching on the Conscience

"Deep within his conscience man discovers a law which he has not laid upon himself but which he must obey. Its voice, ever calling him to love and to do what is good and to avoid evil, tells him inwardly at the right moment: do this, shun that. For man has in his heart a law inscribed by God. His dignity lies in observing this law, and by it he will be judged. His conscience is man's most secret core, and his sanctuary. There he is alone with God whose voice echoes in his depths." (*Gaudium et Spes*, par. 16)

> All who have sinned apart from the law will also perish apart from the law, and all who have sinned under the law will be judged by the law. For it is not the hearers of the law who are righteous in God's sight, but the doers of the law who are justified. When Gentiles, who do not possess the law, do instinctively what the law requires, these, though not

having the law, are a law to themselves. They show that what the law requires is written on their hearts, to which their own *conscience* also bears witness; and their conflicting thoughts will accuse or perhaps excuse them on the day when, according to my gospel, God through Jesus Christ, will judge the secret thoughts of all. (Rom. 2:12-16; italics added)

Paul says here that the conscience indicates the presence of God's moral law in all of humanity, not just in Jews or Christians. Paul does not, however, specifically say that the conscience equals the voice of God within us.

It seems clear that only humans have consciences. We might have a kitten born in our house, and speak to it and demonstrate fine moral practices to it, but it will nonetheless become a cat, driven by instincts to catch and kill mice, lap milk, and purr. Only the human, as Darwin points out, can be moved to complete self-sacrifice by the word "ought." So returning to our primary question: Where do we get our conscience from? It seems that the capacity for being a moral agent is part of our uniquely created human *nature,* whereas the content of that morality is filled by our *nurture.*

When Does the Conscience Address Us?

As I have noted earlier, the conscience addresses us about moral issues, not questions of fashion or taste or scientific fact. We can't say, for instance, that it is wrong to have a miscarriage, to grow apple trees, or to like paintings by Gauguin. Those are not moral issues. The conscience does not speak to us about taste in music or art. The conscience doesn't help us predict the direction of stock-market activity. Clearly, there are some things about which the conscience is not qualified to speak. The conscience addresses strictly moral choices and deeds.

Suneidesis

This is the New Testament Greek term that we translate as "conscience." The literal basis of this term is to "know together." The Latin, from which we get our English word, has the same basis: *con* (with) *science* (knowing). For the Greeks, the conscience was at the center of a person. Conscience was seen as a witness within the self who reports and reflects on what it sees. There is evidence that some Greeks examined their consciences daily, rebuking themselves for failures and praising themselves for successes. Saint Paul knew this Greek tradition, and he built on it when he wrote to the early churches.

The conscience has a time-related aspect. It can address us about moral choices and deeds in the past or the present, and it can provide us with guidance for the future. The conscience can address things we have done, are doing, or might do. When it does so, it may positively clear us of guilt, or it may negatively convict us. David explains how the conscience worked for him before and after he confessed his sin in Psalm 32.

> Happy are those whose transgression is forgiven, whose sin is
>   covered.
> Happy are those to whom the Lord imputes no iniquity, and in
>   whose spirit there is no deceit.
> While I kept silence, my body wasted away through my groaning all
>   day long. For day and night your hand was heavy upon me; my
>   strength was dried up as by the heat of summer.
> Then I acknowledged my sin to you, and I did not hide my iniquity;
>   I said, "I will confess my transgressions to the LORD," and you
>   forgave the guilt of my sin. (Ps. 32:1-5)

In David's case, the conscience brought about physical distress when it reminded him of his sin. But the result was the appropriate one: repentance. The conscience can work on us about our past, bothering us until we acknowledge our sin. The Christian disciple then can confess, be forgiven, and go forward with a cleansed conscience. Or it may be that the conscience helps us realize that there is no sin present, and therefore nothing to confess. As it works toward the future, the conscience helps us imagine who we could become, and what we would feel like if we do the act we contemplate. It might set up a little distress within us as we sense and think about the person we perceive ourselves to be versus the one we will be if we do the act. Or it might please us to think that this is who we might become.

Adiaphora

This Greek term means: things that carry little weight or importance. Problems arise when we give *adiaphora* more weight or importance than they deserve.

Violating the conscience is serious business, and it sets off internal conflict. The conscience can create a battle within. What ought we to do? Who should we become? The question that the conscience raises is one of moral self-identity. We constantly choose the self we arc becoming, and the conscience constantly asks us whether that self is the morally correct one. Joy and peace are the results of a good conscience.

Is the Conscience Always Right?

No. Having a clear conscience might not mean that what we are doing is right. Instead, it may mean that the conscience itself is not right. It may be that the moral software that our culture or genetics has installed is defective. The conscience's programming is written by culture on the brain, and the programming can be faulty. Fixing it might require the ministration of the Holy Spirit, the Christian community, and perhaps a therapist. In any case, our consciences will never be perfect, since no human conscience is equal to the conscience of Christ.

The conscience can malfunction by being either too strict or too lax. For instance, when Paul talks to the Corinthians about eating food sacrificed to idols (1 Cor. 8), he says that the consciences of those who won't eat the meat are too strict. Paul then acknowledges that there really is no such thing as another god, and so the meat sacrificed to these fictitious beings is like the meat of any other animal. Nonetheless, the Corinthian Christians who realized this and ate the meat sacrificed to these idols offended those who believed that there really was something different about that meat. So Paul asks the meat eaters to abstain — out of respect for those whose consciences would not allow them to eat. Paul's great concern for communal peace led him to restrict the conscience of some in order to maintain good relationships with others. So one's conscience is not only an internalized moral norm that must be followed, but it is also a socialized view and practice. Paul's example of the sacrificial meat shows that we should not simply do what we believe to be correct without regard for someone else's conscience. We need to accommodate ourselves to the consciences of other individuals and other communities, as Jesus accommodated himself to our humanness and Paul accommodated himself to both Jews and Greeks.

The problem of a too-strict conscience is real, and can occur in two ways. It may be that someone thinks that an amoral issue is really a moral one. Here again, the Bible mentions just such a case. In 1 Timothy 4:1-5, Paul talks about "hypocritical liars" who "forbid people to marry, and order them to abstain from certain foods, which God created to be received with thanksgiving. . . ." Clearly, these "hypocritical liars" have lied about what is immoral. They claimed that marriage or eating certain foods was immoral. They were wrong, as are those today who want to load up more rules on themselves and other believers than they should.

The other way in which the conscience can be too strict is by weighing a slight infraction as if it were a grave sin. Let's say a son ignores his mother when she has asked him to clean up the kitchen. If his conscience gives him a little jab, that is good. But if his conscience troubles him deeply, and for a long time, it has become a mechanism that is overheated.

What Makes the Christian Conscience Unique?

In one sense, all Christians must have a clear conscience. That is because we stand before God as innocent in Christ. Nothing can convict us, not even our own conscience. As far as sin is concerned, we have been made spotless. As St. Paul writes, "Who will bring a charge against those whom God has chosen? Not God, who acquits! Who will pronounce judgment? Not Christ, who died, or rather rose again; not Christ, who is at God's right hand and pleads our cause!" (Rom. 8:33-34). Forgiveness is the conscience cleanser. We may — and even should — feel guilty for sins that we have committed, but we are not condemned for them. "There is no condemnation for those who are in Christ Jesus!" (Rom. 8:1).

Moral or Amoral?

Today other issues may seem moral when they are really amoral. For instance, the opposite case from the one mentioned in 1 Timothy is sometimes thought to be immoral. That is, some seem to think that it is immoral to remain single rather than to marry and have children. But while it is true that it may be more common to marry, it is certainly not morally wrong to remain single. So there should be no feeling of guilt for remaining single nor any implicit moral rule that all must marry.

Missionaries have sometimes made mistakes about these kinds of things. Some, for example, have insisted that new converts wear certain kinds of clothes or use certain kinds of music in worship. They are mistaken because these are not moral issues.

The conscience, however, continues to address Christians on the matter of sins (plural). Upon conversion, the conscience becomes a witness to the morality of Christ, which is sometimes in contrast to social or family norms. The conscience is a guide that asks us whether the thing we have done or may do follows the path of faith. And the farther we walk with God, the more sensitive our conscience becomes, since we can hear God better if we have been listening carefully throughout our journey. This creates the irony of the well-developed Christian conscience: the more attuned to the conscience one becomes, the more readily it bites. The conscience of a person who has been walking with and listening to the Spirit of Christ for many years will be troubled by a very small wrong, whereas a new Christian or nonbeliever may not hear the voice of conscience at all. My mother, for example, is a life-long Christian, and her conscience now troubles her if she thinks that she said even one word that caused offense to someone else. A less sensitive conscience would likely not even realize that her word had caused offense, let alone find it troubling.

A Caution

Regretting an action is not enough; contrition is required. Regret is simply feeling bad about something you've done and wishing you hadn't done it. Contrition is taking responsibility for the deed and seeking to repair it. Contrition recognizes that our character is distorted by the evil that we do. When we recognize this and seek to undo the evil, we have become contrite.

A well-developed Christian conscience also becomes able to judge the customs of the culture it is part of. It may conclude that some things that are permitted in the culture should not be permissible among Christians, or it may judge that some things that do not follow the social mores of the culture should in fact be permitted. In the early church, for example, Christians took in orphans and cared for the sick to a far greater extent than did their neighbors throughout the Roman Empire, where the custom was to expose unwanted babies — especially female ones — to the elements. Those early Christians refused to leave babies where they could die or be taken away by animals. A study of the church's history can be useful here. As the church has existed throughout various ages and cultures, it has developed an ethic that surpasses that of any one culture.

The conscience is not the only standard by which a Christian judges her action, but it is an important one. The standard by which the conscience itself is judged is the law of God as found in Scripture and as understood by the church. God — not our conscience nor the judgment of any other person — is our ultimate judge. It is in this way that we can best understand Jesus' admonition: "Do not judge, or you, too, will be judged. For in the same way you judge others, you will be judged . . ." (Matt. 7:1-2). We know that the final standard of judgment is God's, and one day he will judge the living and the dead. Saint Paul points out how little the judgment of others may relate to the judgment of God: "I care very little if I am judged by you or by any human court; indeed, I do not even judge myself. My conscience is clear, but that does not make me innocent. It is the Lord who judges me" (1 Cor. 4:3-4).

In a sense, the well-developed Christian conscience permits us to be risk-takers. Christians know that our sins are covered in Christ. Therefore, we need not be paralyzed when confronting issues of moral ambiguity. It may be that in spite of our best thoughts and efforts, we do what is wrong. If that is the case, grace is sufficient for that sin as well. "There is no condemnation for those who are in Christ Jesus!"

Ending Questions

1. None of our deeds, no matter how good, are sufficient to make us right with God. May a Christian, nonetheless, have a clear conscience?
2. The conscience can go wrong in a number of ways: too strict, too lax, too judgmental of others, and so forth. Can you think of examples for each?
3. Does Paul's exhortation to the meat-eaters of Corinth mean that Christians must all squeeze into the mold of those in the community who have the strictest conscience?

Works Cited and Further Reading

Bretzke, James T. *A Morally Complex World: Engaging Contemporary Moral Theology.* Collegeville, MN: Liturgical Press, 2004.

Callahan, Sidney. *In Good Conscience: Reason and Emotion in Moral Decision Making.* San Francisco: HarperCollins, 1991.

Hauser, Marc. *Moral Minds: How Nature Designed Our Universal Sense of Right and Wrong.* New York: HarperCollins, 2006.

Hogan, Linda. *Confronting the Truth: Conscience in the Catholic Tradition.* New York: Paulist Press, 2001.

O'Connell, Timothy. "An Understanding of Conscience." In *Conscience,* edited by Charles Curran. New York: Paulist Press, 2004.

Shin, Joyce S. "Accommodating the Other's Conscience." *Journal of the Society of Christian Ethics* 28, no. 1 (2008): 4-23.

Smedes, Lewis. Class notes.

CHAPTER SEVEN

Moral Norms

"I'M GOING TO tell Mom."

This little refrain comes from the lips of children in many languages, but it is really a profound moral statement. It acknowledges that something may be wrong, that there is a moral standard in play, and that the source of that moral standard is Mother. We all have sources for our morality, and most do begin with our parents. In fact, some people still use their parents as their moral standard long after they have left home. For example, "Boy, if Dad ever heard about this...." And if your parents are good moral models, this can be a pretty good way to set your moral compass.

There are norms for different things. For example, there are aesthetic norms that apply to music and art; norms exist for etiquette that apply to table manners; norms for rituals that prescribe correct worship in each religious tradition; the norms found in civil laws that vary from nation to nation. This chapter will focus on moral norms: those that show us which acts are right and wrong, or good and evil. Norms give guidance in advance. We could not live without them, nor could we pretend to create new moral standards of behavior from day to day.

In this chapter I will look at the sources from which people derive their moral norms. Another way of saying this is to ask the question: Where do my moral obligations come from? Obligations are things we must do. So where do we get the notions we have about our moral obligations, the *shoulds* of life? Some possibilities for the sources of moral obligation include: *myself, society, nature's law,* the *church,* a *universal principle,* and *divine revelation.* The preceding chapter on conscience addressed one source; in this chapter I will treat the first five mentioned here. Divine revelation will be the subject of the next chapter.

The Self as Moral Norm

If pursuing my own happiness is the norm by which I live, that standard is called *egoism.* The novelist Ayn Rand was an advocate of egoism. She posed egoism as a contrast to altruism, and she preferred egoism. She saw altruism as advocating that "any action taken for the benefit of others is good, and any action taken for one's own benefit is evil. Thus the beneficiary of an action is the only criterion of moral value — and so long as the beneficiary is anybody other than oneself, anything goes" (Rand, p. vii). Seen in this way, she has a point. Why should the only criterion for the goodness of an act be the fact that it serves someone else? She adds: "If a man accepts the ethics of altruism, his first concern is not how to live his life, but how to sacrifice it. . . . Altruism erodes men's capacity to grasp the value of an individual life; it reveals a mind from which the reality of a human being has been wiped out" (Rand, p. 27). Egoists like Rand insist that we are our own masters, and that we should not be mastered by anyone else. We alone know what our desires are, and others know what theirs are. If we meddle with others, we may do them more harm than good. So it is best that each pursue his or her own desires.

But the views of both egoism and altruism as depicted by Rand are extremes. Jesus, for example, does not advocate the kind of altruism that Rand mentions. When Jesus answered the question of what the greatest commandment of the law was, he did not say that we should "love our neighbor *more than* ourselves." He said that we should "love our neighbor *as* ourselves." In affirming this commandment, Jesus did not advocate self-abuse or abasement. Rather, he affirmed that others merit the same respect and honor that we do.

Pure egoism would also be difficult to actually practice. For example, what if what I most want for myself is to have a friend? Could

I be a friend to anyone if my only interest was focused on myself and I had no interest in the friend for her own sake? Egoism can also be self-defeating, since getting the best for ourselves often requires cooperation, which by definition entails giving up some of what we desire. A further objection to egoism is that it does not recognize that we are social selves. We are not merely individuals; we live among other people who are embedded in community. In other words, the anthropological assumption of individualism that underlies egoism is questionable.

Another way our selves may be an ethical norm is to focus on our emotions. In this case, when we make a moral judgment, what we are really saying is: "I feel dislike for what you have done." This ethical norm says that the individual's emotions are the standards by which we can judge morality. If it feels pleasing, it is okay; if it gives us a negative sensation, it is not permissible. This is called *ethical emotivism:* it proposes that when we say that something is right or wrong, what we are really doing is expressing the emotions that we feel about that act.

This position also has its problems. First, our emotions about something can be wrongheaded. For example, you might be very envious of the guy who marries the beautiful and wealthy young woman you had your eye on, so you may hate her new husband. But he did no wrong, and the marriage might turn out to be beneficial for him, her, and many others — in spite of the emotions you might have about it. In fact, your misplaced envy might motivate you to do something evil, like murdering the husband or stalking the woman. Second, moral statements are of a different kind than emotive expressions of preference. Saying "I feel dislike toward greasy bacon" is quite different from saying "I feel dislike toward ethnic cleansing." We can have feelings about a great many things, and the feelings we have about moral issues are not equal to those we have about many other subjects. We cannot argue about tastes: for example, you can't say that my taste for beets is wrong because you hate beets. My tastes are mine, and yours are yours. As the old saying goes, "Regarding tastes, there is no dispute." This is also true of emotions: for instance, you cannot rationally argue that I am wrong to be weeping. Therefore, moral reasoning or argumentation is impossible if the standard is that of emotive judgments alone.

Society/Culture as Moral Norm

The *Oxford English Dictionary* defines "culture" this way: "The distinctive ideas, customs, social behaviour, products, or way of life of a particular society, people, or period. Hence: a society or group characterized by such customs. . . ." Culture is, in short, the set of meanings that humans construct within their environment. It is the cultivation of all aspects of life. For example, whereas all peoples have children, the way groups of people raise their children varies from culture to culture. Or, whereas all people construct buildings, the architecture in one culture may differ considerably from that of another. Culture includes what we see in the media, what our friends and families customarily do, and the ways we shape our physical environment. There are, for example, river cultures that are different from cultures of the plains. There are cultures that are Arab, but infused with Western media, and other Arab cultures in which few or no Western media are allowed. These elements of our culture are almost like the air we breathe. If you were raised in the United States, it probably would not occur to you to embrace someone you hardly know with a kiss, or burp voluminously after a meal, or take your shoes off and put on slippers before entering a home. These are cultural norms from other societies and cultures.

Besides having different norms, different cultures have different practices. For example, aged Eskimos would take a long walk out into the cold to effectively commit suicide, thus alleviating their family's need to provide for them. In China, by way of contrast, the aged are honored in such a way that the young will give up their food for the elders. But do these differences in practice mean that all moral norms are relative to their society? I don't think so. Rather, it may mean that there are moral norms for all, such as respect for life, but that they are *practiced* quite differently in one society than in another. The willing death of the elderly Eskimos protects the fragile life of their community, whereas the communal life in China respects the life of the aged more than that of its youth. In both cases, there is a moral norm of respect for life.

What I hope to show here is that differing practices do not negate the existence of moral norms; instead, it may be that differing practices follow the same norm. Or it may be that some moral norms are regularly broken. For example, assume that you and everyone you hang around with steals from time to time. This fact would not mean that there is no such thing as theft; it would mean that you and your friends are all thieves. In more academic terminology, social relativism does not require ethical relativism.

To say that culture is the source of norms seems to imply that morality is relative to culture, engendering what is called "cultural relativism." In cultural relativism, moral norms become the names your society uses for customs it approves of. Relativism claims that the following statements all amount to the same thing: "It is good, it is our habit, and it is approved by our society." Norms vary widely from culture to culture. For example, among the Kwakiutl of the Pacific Northwest, all deaths must be avenged, even if the death was brought about by disease or accident (Benedict, pp. 59-82). Another famous case is reported by Herodotus. The Persian king Darius asked about the burial practices of the Greeks. They responded that they honored their dead by cremating them. He then asked the Asian Callatians, who were also in his court, how they took care of the dead bodies of their citizens. They responded by saying that they honored their dead by eating the corpses. Each group was horrified by the practice of the other group (Pojman, p. 48).

There are other practical problems with ethical relativism that need to be addressed, such as, who is the group that sets the norms? For example, you could set up a commune that enforced the distribution of food, medical services, and marriage partners on the basis of hair color. Redheads get first choice, blonds get second choice, brown-haired people are next, and the black-haired go last. Would it be morally permissible to enforce this distribution system on your group? What if the group grew to 100, then 1,000, then 1,000,000? What if your group became a 51 percent majority in one region? Could you then vote in

Case Study

Jerry and Lori wonder if they should even worry about this issue of a new house. They earned the money for it honestly; they pay their share to the church; and they enjoy the lake. Where are they getting the notion that the purchase of a new condo is something that relates to moral norms? Many of their friends simply advise, "You earned it, you deserve it." But is this earn/spend ethic really the whole story?

this norm as the standard for the other 49 percent of the people there? Another way of putting the question is this: If morals are relative to the group, what constitutes the group?

Another problem with moral relativism is that it is impossible for the majority to make ethical errors. If the majority of the group says that *XYZ* is morally permissible, so it is. A reformer who wishes to challenge the legitimacy of the action *Y* has no way of appealing to something outside the group itself. Say, for instance, that the majority of one group of people agrees that female circumcision is right. If you are an ethical relativist, you would have to simply say, "Okay." If the people are doing what is right according to their cultural standards, you cannot either judge the practice or argue about it. If you did argue or judge, you would be admitting that there is a norm beyond your culture to which you appeal. But that would mean that you can no longer consider yourself an ethical relativist.

A problem does arise when people presume that the cultural norms from their society are in fact universal and moral norms. In other words, the question of what is right and wrong is not the same as the question of what is culturally appropriate. Upon my arrival at a Japanese home when I visited that country, I bowed (in keeping with what I knew about Japanese culture), but then I entered the house with my shoes on (since I hadn't learned about that part of Japanese culture yet). I do not believe my shoed entrance into that home was a sin. It was instead a cultural error brought about by innocent ignorance. However, if I later decided to tramp into that house with my dirty shoes on, I believe it would have been a moral wrong. In that case my intent would have been to dishonor the lady of the house. Some norms are cultural, not moral.

Nature and the Law of Nature

Beginning no later than the Greeks, humans have thought that nature itself serves as a moral standard for humans. Aristotle believed that living "according to nature" meant to fulfill the natural destiny that each person has, and to develop the virtues necessary to do so. In the

Christian tradition, Thomas Aquinas (1225-74) put this idea to use in his theology. It has sometimes been called "natural law," meaning that the moral law can be derived from nature. The basic assumption of natural law in Aquinas is that there is one Creator God who made the whole world in an orderly way. Humans, by studying nature, can determine what the divine order for the world is. This order takes the name of "law," and there are different kinds of law.

The *eternal law* includes all of the order that God places in the world: it includes everything from the law of gravity to traffic laws. Within this great order are norms that show humans how to be made right with God; these are called the *divine law*. A second set of norms is called *natural law*. These laws are accessible to (i.e., can be known by) all humans by virtue of the fact that all people have reasoning abilities. A third set of norms is *civil law*. These laws show how the natural law can be applied to particular societies. So, for example, the civil laws of ancient Israel and modern Italy will not be the same, but according to Aquinas, both must derive from natural law in order to be legitimate. Perhaps the following chart will clarify this.

In the chart below, you will notice that under natural law there are three categories. These three categories, according to Aquinas, represent the three aspects of human nature: we are material substance, animal, and rational. Each aspect of our nature has a goal.

"I Didn't Know"?

A therapist once told me that he had a session with a sister and brother who were engaged in incest. When confronted about this, they exclaimed with surprise: "We didn't know we weren't supposed to do that!"

Does this response seem possibly true?

....

A. By virtue of being a substance,

                we desire self preservation.

....

B. By virtue of being an animal,

                we desire to procreate.

....

C. By virtue of being a rational being,

                we desire to know God and his world.

Since we are rational beings, we can discover the nature of our world — and the right within it. When we do the things that are in accord with our nature, we will do the right. When we act counter to our nature, we do wrong. This may be abstract. To express it concretely, when we eat, we do right by our nature since as substances we desire self-preservation. When we have marital sex, we do right by our nature since we desire to procreate. When we read Scripture, we do right by our nature since we desire to know God.

ETERNAL LAW
By which God ordered
the universe

Divine Law
— which leads
  to salvation

Natural Law
— devoted to human
  happiness
— order of nature
— order of reason

Civil/Positive Law
Derived from natural
law and applied to
specific communities

The most useful part of Aquinas's theory is probably the assumption of the rationality of humans. Belief in an objective moral code implies belief in a common, rational, human nature. According to Aquinas, all humans possess a rational nature and can thus know moral truth. For example, by reason you can see that killing another human being is wrong; it destroys another being who is not only substantial and animal-like, but rational. A bit of reasoned reflection quickly yields the idea that murder is then wrong among all humans. You can see that natural law is a stronger ground for obligation than is social convention or egoism.

We can tell if a civil law is moral by whether it comports with natural law. For Aquinas, a civil law that did not correspond to natural law was no law at all. If civil laws follow from natural law, they are legitimate; if they are contradictory to it, they are illegitimate. However, this view of the legitimacy of civil law is problematic. For example, the laws of apartheid that separated racial groups in South Africa were legal, and they corresponded to what many white South Africans thought were natural distinctions between races. But, in fact, they were immoral. They wrongly distinguished people on the basis of their race, and they bestowed rights and duties on that basis rather than on the basis of the common humanity of all.

The Protestant reception of natural law has challenged its optimism. It is, Protestants argue, rather optimistic to think that all humans will use their reason rightly, and thus discover the truths of natural law. Instead, people will often use their reason to justify their wrongdoing. Or they will "suppress the truth by their own wickedness" (Rom. 1:18), pay no attention to it, or deny its validity. In short, while most Protestants agree that there is a moral order that derives from God, they doubt that most humans are apt to mind that order — due to the effects of sin in our world and within each person.

Other philosophers have criticized the movement that natural law makes between the natural and the moral, that is, between the *is* and the *ought.* They argue that, though we may know what something is like, and even what it is for, we may not then presume that we also know how it *ought* to be. The most famous example of this problem is perhaps that of sexuality expressed in the papal encyclical *Humanae Vitae* (On Human Life). This encyclical follows natural law regarding sexuality. Accordingly, sexuality has a purpose among humans just as it does among other animals: the creation of new life. Therefore, natural law advocates argue that sexual acts that do not have the potential to create new life are illegitimate. In this view, even married couples who have sexual intercourse simply for its pleasure are sinning against natural law if they use contraception.

A third critique arises as a result of changes that have occurred in modern times. When Aquinas wrote about natural law, all of Europe was culturally "Christian," and nearby Muslims shared in the common heritage of Abraham. Most people thought about things in much the same way: that is, their worldview was very similar. Today we recognize that people in other times and cultures think quite differently about things than we do. This is not to say that they do not use reason; rather, it is that their basic presuppositions about life can be quite different from our own. For example, in many countries women are expected to be veiled and to keep quiet. That is a norm of those societies, a norm that is not observed in the Western world. So we would now ask Aquinas: What is rational and natural here? Is it the rationality that buttresses the norms of culture A or B or C?

This has been quite a long discussion of natural law. But since it

Reason as the Source of Law

In Aquinas's time, using reason as the source of law was quite radical. At that time people thought that the king was the source of law. Aquinas's ideas were later used to challenge the divine right of kings to make laws.

was the standard of obligation for European cultures for centuries, I think it is worth examining in full.

The Church as Moral Norm

It is perhaps fitting to mention the church as a source for moral norms immediately after discussing natural law. The church, especially the Roman Catholic Church, sees itself as the institution that has the clearest insight into the law of God, since it has been entrusted with truth from God. Based on the teachings and practices of the apostles, the church has always sought to guide Christian disciples in the moral life. In fact, it is not only the Roman Catholic Church, but all church denominations, that do this. Rare is the preacher who does not adjure his congregants to do what is morally right and abstain from evil. Rarer still is the congregation that does not have a set of moral standards for its members. Sometimes these standards are implicit, and sometimes they are explicit; but they are certainly present. For example, some churches read the Ten Commandments in the worship service, while others do not. But all churches assume that they should be followed.

The church is a community that all Christians are part of. Since it is a social group as well as a religious one, it sets standards for the morality of its members at a social level as well as a theological one. For example, someone may say, "She is not a good Catholic," or someone else might say, "That Baptist politician brings shame on our church." Here community standards are tightly tied to religious communities. Catholics or Baptists should look and act like the community they are part of. Within the Roman Catholic tradition, the church's role as moral teacher is specifically set forth. The following quotations are from the *Catechism of the Catholic Church:*

> 2032 The Church, the "pillar and bulwark of the truth," has received this solemn command of Christ from the apostles to announce the saving truth. To the Church belongs the right always and everywhere to announce moral principles, including those pertaining to the social order, and to make judgments on any human affairs to the extent that

they are required by the fundamental rights of the human person or the salvation of souls.

2033 The *Magisterium of the Pastors of the Church* in moral matters is ordinarily exercised in catechesis and preaching, with the help of the works of theologians and spiritual authors. Thus from generation to generation, under the aegis and vigilance of the pastors, the "deposit" of Christian moral teaching has been handed on, a deposit composed of a characteristic body of rules, commandments, and virtues proceeding from faith in Christ and animated by charity. Alongside the Creed and the Our Father, the basis for this catechesis has traditionally been the Decalogue, which sets out the principles of moral life valid for all men.

2246 It is a part of the Church's mission "to pass moral judgments even in matters related to politics, whenever the fundamental rights of man or the salvation of souls requires it. The means, the only means, [the Church] may use are those which are in accord with the Gospel and the welfare of all men according to the diversity of times and circumstances." (interior quote from *Gaudium et Spes* 76, par. 5)

The Roman Catholic Church is quite clear on matters about which many evangelical churches are not. That church body claims a special role as moral guide in the lives of church members, as well as in society. It explicitly claims this special role and tradition of moral instruction on the basis of its reception of the teachings of Christ and his apostles. The Catholic Church is at liberty to announce moral principles whenever those principles affect human rights or salvation.

Roman Catholics have a substantial body of moral teaching to turn to. There are moral instructions on any issue you can think of: war, abortion, business practices, roles of women, and so on. These teachings come in a wide variety of formats, and they have differing degrees of authority. For example, if the pope speaks ex cathedra on an issue, his teaching is believed to be infallible. (I should note that the pope has never promulgated an infallible moral teaching, only doctrinal ones.) If he circulates an encyclical to all of the Catholic Church, that teaching is authoritative and official, but not infallible. If bishops circulate a teaching, it is usually referred to as a "letter," such as the one sent by the U.S. bishops entitled "Economic Justice for All."

A Universal Principle

When can or should norms become universalized? That is, when can we say, "I would not do that, nor should anyone else." Philosopher Immanuel Kant (1724-1804) proposed that ethics must be based on a principle from which there can be no exceptions. He called this a "categorical imperative," which he distinguished from a "conditional imperative." The conditional imperative is an if/then imperative. For example, if you want to keep your house safe, then you should buy a security system ("if . . . then"). On the other hand, a categorical imperative is simply a command, for example, "Keep your promise!" For Kant, there are no exceptions to categorical imperatives. His standard for action is to do the things yourself that you would want to have all people do. For example, you might wish to break a promise, but unless you permit all people to break their promises, you may not break it. Kant says, "There is . . . but one categorical imperative, namely, this: Act only on the maxim whereby you can at the same time will that it should become a universal law."

Many norms, even good ones, should not be made universal. For example, if I say that I am going to give up meat and become a vegetarian because I will save the lives of animals and experience better health, may I then say, "You should do that, too"? No, this norm is not obligatory on all. Some norms are universal, such as those found in the second table of the Ten Commandments. But while these commands prohibit harm, they do not specify the degree of good that we should do, nor how we should accomplish it. Many "shoulds" are not only things that we may not do, but matters of personal ability or voca-

Case Study

John and Dee's church has a strong pro-life stance. It believes that life begins at conception and ends when there is no longer a brain wave. But as John and Dee look at their mother, they see a gradual process of dying underway. The problem is not so much that she is now alive, but that she will be dead. It is the process of her dying in which she becomes less and less the person they all knew.

tion. Perhaps I should become a doctor who saves lives in Africa, but you should become a dancer and entertain us.

Therefore, we are not necessarily subject to the "shoulds" of others. If someone says, "Well, I would have done such and such," that doesn't always mean that this is what *you* should do. Certainly all of us should do no harm, and sometimes we should do some good. But choosing which good things you should do, and which I should do — as well as the way you or I should do them — may vary widely given our abilities and circumstances. We are not capable of doing all possible good things; nor are we responsible to do so. We are not God. We are particular people in particular places, times, and vocations — all of which is good. God has placed us in our particular circumstances to serve him and our neighbors.

Types of Norms

There are three types of norms:

Obligatory
those things we must do

Permissible
those things we may do

Supererogatory
those good things we might do that go beyond what is required or necessary, beyond our obligation to perform them

Conflict of Norms

Our examination of norms must acknowledge that norms may not always agree with one another. For example, your mother might say *A,* your society says *B,* and your emotions say *C.* Conflicts between sympathy and morality may also occur. For example, the norms of Huck Finn's social morality taught him that slaves should be returned to their legal masters; but his sympathy said that his black friend, Jim, must be freed. His good passions ran counter to the established morality and law of his time. On the other hand, those working for the Nazis had to squelch all feeling of sympathy in order to effectively kill off Jews and gypsies in order to follow a vicious civil norm. From this arises a standard critique of norm-based ethics: that it does not account for sympathy.

Nonetheless, I conclude that there are norms that each one of us adheres to, whether consciously or not. And it is good that we do. We cannot invent right and wrong anew every day. Rather than seeing the conflict of norms or the absence of sympathy within them as insuperable challenges, we should appreciate the limitations of norm-based ethics. The fact that you are now more conscious of the sources of moral norms makes it likely that you will be better equipped to ask and answer questions of right and wrong, and then to identify your own source for those answers.

Ending Questions

1. In your own words, define what a moral norm is.
2. List several reasons why *self* is not a good moral norm to live by.
3. Why would a societal/cultural norm not be considered a universal moral norm?
4. Explain the difference between *divine law, natural law,* and *civil law* as presented by the author.
5. How, according to civil and natural laws, might apartheid have been legitimated?
6. How does sin affect our ability to live rightly under natural law?
7. Why is it difficult for the church to be the "moral teacher" in determining our moral standards for living?

Works Cited and Further Reading

Benedict, Ruth. "Anthropology and the Abnormal." *The Journal of General Psychology* 10 (1934): 59-82.

Catechism of the Catholic Church. Rome: Libreria Editrice Vaticana, 1997.

Kant, Immanuel. *Fundamental Principles of the Metaphysics of Morals.* Translated by T. K. Abbott. Charleston, SC: Biblio Bazaar LLC, 1898.

Kreeft, Peter. *A Refutation of Moral Relativism: Interviews with an Absolutist.* San Francisco: Ignatius Press, 1999.

Krier Mich, Marvin L. *Catholic Social Teaching and Movements.* Mystic, CT: Twenty-Third Publications, 2001.

Meilaender, Gilbert. *The Freedom of a Christian: Grace, Vocation, and the Meaning of Our Humanity.* Grand Rapids: Brazos Press, 2006.

Midgley, Mary. *Can't We Make Moral Judgments?* New York: St. Martin's Press, 1991.

Pojman, Louis P. *How Should We Live?* Belmont, CA: Thomson/Wadsworth, 2005.

Rand, Ayn. *The Virtue of Selfishness.* New American Library, 1964.

Smedes, Lewis B. *Choices: Making Right Decisions in a Complex World.* New York: HarperCollins, 1991.

CHAPTER EIGHT

Biblical Norms

THE BIBLE SETS standards for us. In fact, one major theme within the Bible is the story of our failure to meet God's standard — and then God's solution for meeting that standard through Christ. While it is certain that we cannot earn salvation by keeping God's law, the law nevertheless remains in force even after Christ has satisfied its demands. Jesus himself says:

> Do not suppose that I have come to abolish the law and the prophets; I did not come to abolish, but to complete. Truly I tell you: so long as heaven and earth endure, not a letter, not a dot, will disappear from the law until all that must happen has happened. Anyone therefore who sets aside even the least of the law's demands, and teaches other to do the same, will have the lowest place in the kingdom of Heaven, whereas anyone who keeps the law, and teaches others to do so, will rank high in the kingdom of Heaven. I tell you, unless you show yourselves far better than the scribes and Pharisees, you can never enter the kingdom of Heaven. (Matt. 5:17-20)

The first major law texts of the Bible are found in the book of Exodus. The most famous of these, of course, are the Ten Commandments, which are a part of the "covenant law." This relationship to the covenant shapes their nature and intent. Notice that the law section in the book of Exodus follows the account of the Exodus of the Israelites, which was the sign of God's great deliverance. By means of the Exodus, the people of Israel were liberated from captivity to a false lord, Pharaoh, and they were brought into a freedom in which they could serve the true Lord — Yahweh. The formula of the covenant thus begins with the words: "I am the LORD your God, who brought you out of the land of Egypt, out of the land of slavery" (Exod. 20:2). In saying this, God first establishes the relationship between the law-giver and the recipients of the law. The recipients are those whom God has delivered from slavery, those whom he has saved. Thus the law cannot be understood as the tool we can use to pry loose God's salvation, since that salvation has already occurred. It must be for other reasons that God gives his already saved people the law.

Roles of Covenant Law

During the Reformation period (beginning in 1517 with Martin Luther), John Calvin emphasized that there are three distinct roles for God's law. The first role of the law is to show us our sins, and in so doing to demonstrate our need for a savior. This may seem to contradict what I just said about the law coming after salvation; but it really confirms it. For those who haven't yet been delivered from their bondage to sin, the law presents that need in stark terms. For believers, hearing the law can cut us deeply and remind us of the ugliness and waywardness of our lives. It reminds us that we must constantly turn to our Savior, who has delivered us from sin, and ask for deliverance from those sins that continue to haunt us. Thus the law shows believers how badly we need a Savior on a daily basis, and it shows nonbelievers their vital, once-for-all need for the gift of salvation.

The second role of the law is to serve as a guide for civil society. God brought Israel into a land that was promised to their forefather Abraham. This land was to be the inheritance of God's people, the place where

John Calvin (1509-1564)

Calvin was a French-born Renaissance scholar who accepted the Protestant faith. He dedicated his life to interpreting the Bible (which he read in its original languages of Hebrew and Greek) and establishing a Reformed community in the French-speaking Swiss city of Geneva.

His ideas live on in Reformed and Presbyterian churches, as well as in Western political thought.

they displayed God's justice and holiness to the nations. How could Israel display God's justice? By keeping the law. For example, God's law shows that a just nation is one in which the poor are honored and the widows are cared for; it uses fair weights and measures; it respects the marriages and property of others, and so on. Covenant law served as a guide for ancient Israel, and in some ways it continues to serve as a guide for justice today.

The third use of the law, which is most specific to Calvin, is that it serves as a guide for believers, showing them how to live as grateful servants of God. When asked what the greatest of the commandments was, Jesus responded with the command to love God above all (Deut. 6:5) and to love our neighbors as we do ourselves (Lev. 19:18). Both of these are law texts. They show how the redeemed should live. Biblical law serves as the standard for showing love. It answers this question: Since God has delivered us and made us his own, how, then, shall we live?

Love and Justice

The law Jesus cites as the greatest command of all is the command to love. In other words, the fulfillment of the justice demanded by law is love. What is the relationship between love and justice? Is one previous to the other? Is one greater than the other? Typically, Christian theologians have answered that question by saying that justice serves as the basis of love, and love fulfills and goes beyond justice. Let's work through this.

If you are to be married, and are planning your weddings vows, you will likely say something like this: "I promise to love, cherish and honor you, until death parts us." In saying this you set a standard of love for your marriage. What if your fiancé instead said, "I promise not to hurt you, steal from you, or abuse you"? How many people would feel good about entering into a marriage on those terms? In saying this, the fiancé does promise to obey the law: he promises not to harm you or act in a criminal way toward you. But these are clearly minimal standards that are expected of everyone, let alone the person you are marrying. The standard of love that you would expect from a spouse goes well beyond this minimal base of keeping the law. Love entails the desire to seek another's good; love even sacrifices itself for the good of another. Surely, it also implies no intentional harm, which is why spouses who are abusive fall short of the standards of *both* love and justice.

Justice is the bare minimum standard of fair behavior that must occur for love to have a chance, but love goes well beyond the demand of justice. In turn, love demands justice. That is, our desire for someone's good compels us to seek justice for that person. There is no contradiction between love and justice; rather, justice serves as the foundation of love, and love is the fulfillment of justice.

God's Will

"Thy will be done, on earth as it is in heaven." These well-known words from the Lord's Prayer are spoken daily by many Christians. What does "God's will" entail?

First, God's will *performs* things. In Genesis 1 it was God's will that light should emerge from the darkness, and so it was. In the New Testament it was God's will for the second person of the Trinity to become incarnate, and he was. So in this sense, God's will is what God does.

It is also true that God's will *permits* things. For example, given the presence of microbes, it is normal for many people to suffer disease, and sometimes they die. God permits this. The way creation is structured permits both great ills and great goods. It seems that most often we tend to claim that God is unfair when the great ills occur, but we presume that the great goods of health, family, nature, and so forth, are normal. God's will permits a great deal of both good and ill.

Sometimes God's will *prescribes* things. That is, God prescribes what we should do. This view of God's will is seen in biblical law. What should be done, according to God's will, is expressed in God's law. But keep in mind that the law does not equal the fullness of the will of God. As Christian philosopher Caroline Simon notes, "God's intentions are broader than his commands" (Simon, p. 21). The ultimate goal of God's prescription for us is to love, as he loved us. When Christians pray that God's will be done on earth as it is in heaven, they seek a very high standard.

The laws of Scripture have two focuses: how we relate to God and how we relate to other humans and creation. The laws that address our relationship to God are encapsulated in the first commands of the Decalogue: "You shall have no gods before me; you shall not make images; you shall not swear in my name" (Exod. 20:1-7). The first table of the law (commandments 1-5) establishes standards for our relationship with God. It prescribes right behavior for the worship and honor of God. Dozens of laws in the Old Testament, as well as many in the New Testament, specify and clarify just how to keep these commands. These are typically called *religious* (or "cultic") laws.

Another set of laws, those encapsulated in the second half of the Decalogue (commandments 6-10), are directed toward other persons and the creation (Exod. 20:12-17). In those commandments God prescribes that we treat others with honor — as fellow image-bearers. This means, as these laws show, that one-seventh of their time belongs to God, that their marriage is holy, that their property and lives are their own. Again, hundreds of laws in the Old Testament and many in the New Testament expand on these basic precepts, showing what it means in a particular context and guiding us in our own context. The second half of the Decalogue is *moral* law; other laws of this type are moral and civil.

The law in between these two groups in the Decalogue is the Sabbath law (Exod. 20:8-11). It seems to be a bridge between those that are God-related and those that are neighbor-related. The law commands one day of rest during every week. Honoring this law shows that we recognize God as the God of time itself. All time is God's, and all work must be done for God. Yet the command also reminds us that our neighbors, employees, and draft animals are also servants of God, and they also merit rest. We must honor their time and their relationship to God, as we do our own.

Types of Laws

Not all laws in the Bible are moral laws. Theologians have often understood the laws of Scripture under the categories of moral, civil, and ritual. Though this set of categories is imperfect (the Jews themselves did not see them in exactly this way), using these categories to sort through the wide range of biblical laws can be helpful. As I have noted, *moral laws* have the object of creation or humanity in view. They ask, How shall we treat the world and its creatures? This is a broad question, and moral law seeks to provide a broad answer to it.

Civil laws also have humanity and creation in view, but they are more specifically aimed at running a particular society than they are at setting up a moral standard for all of humanity. For example, the Bible talks about what should happen if an animal falls into a pit. Exodus 21:33-34 says: "If a man uncovers a pit or digs one and fails to cover it and an ox or a donkey falls into it, the owner of the pit must pay for the loss; he must pay its owner, and the dead animal will be his." I do not tend to dig many pits, nor do I have an ox or donkey, and I doubt you do either. But I am sure that in ancient Israel this was a very good civil law. They did dig pits, and animals did fall in from time to time. Christians today may well learn from the law by applying the principle behind it to contemporary law.

The Sabbath

How do you honor the Sabbath?

Does your honoring of it recognize that God is the ruler of both your time and that of all other people and creatures?

For instance, the law clearly addresses the need to care for the goods of others. Is there something that I do that puts others' possessions or lives at risk? If so, I should change it. And if my negligence does cause harm, I am responsible for restoration of the lost item. In a way, this law about oxen and donkeys may be parallel to the current legal mandates to carry insurance or provide restitution.

Ritual laws are aimed at the worship of God. They tell the ancient Israelites how to worship God and maintain holiness. Leviticus 19:2 says: "Be holy, for I, the LORD your God, am holy," and the many laws that follow in that chapter are part of what is called the "Holiness Code." Holiness focuses on purity, on being set apart as God's own people. Many of the ritual laws in the Old Testament sound weird to us: "Don't wear cloth made of two materials, don't eat creatures like the lobster, don't eat meat with the blood in it," and so on (Lev. 19). To understand these laws requires some knowledge of the religious rituals practiced in the nations around Israel. It was common, for instance, to think that if the life force of an animal was in the blood, then drinking the blood of an animal would give the person who drank it the power, speed, or agility of that animal. The laws of the Pentateuch will have none of this: they insist on proper sacrifice that is made in the court of the tabernacle, not magical rites.

In general, ritual laws symbolize the requirement of singleness and unity in worship and action. For example, a lobster is a sea creature, but it has legs. It is thus a rather confused creature. Israel was not to be an impure nation: it was to choose the right and not the wrong and not pretend as if there were no difference. So, as a sign of this single-mindedness, Israelites were not permitted to eat lobster.

It is clear that the sacrifice of Jesus removed the need to purify oneself by dietary or other ritual regulations. That is the point of the story in Acts 10, where Peter is told to kill the so-called unclean animals and eat them. From this vision he learned that the mark of holiness was no longer diet or sacrifice, but the presence of the Spirit, who is holy. In the New Testament, the command to be holy nevertheless remains valid. Saint Peter writes, "But you are a chosen race, a royal priesthood, a holy nation, God's own people . . ." (1 Pet. 2:9). It is clear that Peter does not envision continued sacrifice, but he does insist that God's people be holy. Holiness still implies a pure dedication to God and the avoidance of evil.

Levels of Law

Not all biblical laws are equal. For example, the "love your neighbor as yourself" law is clearly bigger and more important than the one about covering up the pit you dug (though that one is implicit in loving your neighbor as yourself). One way to understand these differences is to distinguish among *principles, precepts,* and *rules.*

A *principle* is a moral law that covers the whole range of moral action. I can think of only three of these universal moral principles: love, justice, and holiness. What I mean by this is that, when we con-

Holiness

How can people today be holy? Does it imply avoidance of "worldly" things?

Some churches do this by limiting movie options, or prohibiting drinking, among other things. Do you think this is effective?

Can you be holy and still party?

sider a course of moral action, it is always appropriate to act in love, or justice, or holiness. There is no moral action to which these principles would not apply. Indeed, Jesus summed up the moral law in this very way: Love God above all and love your neighbor as yourself.

A *precept* takes one slice of the morality pie and focuses on it. For example, the command "do not kill" is a precept. It is more specific than the principle of love, and certainly is consistent with it. If you love someone, you will not kill that person. Or stated in the negative, by killing someone you have clearly demonstrated that you do not love that person. Similarly, the other commandments such as "you shall not steal or commit adultery" are actually precepts. They take one portion of the moral pie and give it focus. If you love your neighbor you may not take her material goods, nor corrupt her marriage. Doing these things would contradict the precepts that prohibit theft or adultery, as well as the principle to love your neighbor as yourself.

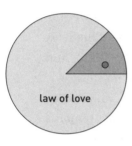

law of love

The principle of the law of love covers the whole pie. A precept such as "Do not steal" covers one slice. A rule such as "Don't use false weights on your scale" is one point within the slice.

Rules are the most specific of the laws. Rules give very concrete instructions about what should be done. For example, Deuteronomy 22:10 says: "Do not plow with an ox and a donkey yoked together." That is a pretty clear rule. This law may relate to holiness (e.g., let's not confuse our use of animals), or it may protect the weaker donkey from being abused by being yoked with the stronger ox. Saint Paul later takes this very concrete agricultural law from Deuteronomy and applies the principle behind it to Christian marriage: "Do not be yoked with an unbeliever" (2 Cor. 6:14).

Let's sum up what we have so far. The principles and precepts of moral law still guide the lives of Christians today, though the rules are often too culturally specific to use directly. Biblical laws are often instructive, but we hardly want Congress to enact them in our modern society. And ritual laws must be seen as antecedents of the demand for holiness that is now available via the Holy Spirit.

Formats for Law

There are two ways to format laws. The first is called *casuistic,* and the second *apodictic.* (For *casuistic,* think of a case study.) The law about covering a pit is an example of the casuistic way of formatting a law. It includes an "if . . . then" formulation, or at least implies it: "*If* a person should leave a pit uncovered and the neighbor's donkey falls into it, *then* the person who dug the pit needs to reimburse the neighbor for the loss of his animal." *Apodictic* laws are those of the second format: they simply tell you what you should or should not do. The Ten Commandments are examples of apodictic laws: do not make idols, do not kill, and so on.

So each law in the Old Testament can be a principle or a precept or a rule; it can have as its focus morality, civil standards, or holiness; and it can be formatted either apodictically or casuistically.

Case Study

John and Dee want to do God's will with regard to Dee's mother. The law of God says, "Honor your parents for this is right." They want to do this, so perhaps the *way* they do it is not crucial. In other words, if they are obeying the principle of love, and the precept of parental honor, the method they follow in doing so may not be that important.

Law in the New Testament

Saint Paul spends a good deal of his writings (especially in the letter to the Galatians) showing how the law can lead the Christian out of grace and back to slavery; but he goes on to insist that the law is good and that obedience to it necessary. He writes: "What then should we say? That the law is sin? By no means! . . . The law is holy, and the commandment is holy and just and good" (Rom. 7:7, 12). Paul clearly believed that all humans are moral creatures. But in Romans 1 and 2 he shows that the morality God demanded through the law has been met with universal immorality among both the Jews and the Gentiles. God's response to this universal immorality is hot anger. Immorality is offensive to the just and holy one. It brings harm to God's relationship with humans, to the relationships among humans, and to the ones between humans and the created world. Christ is called on to remove these offenses and restore these relationships. This restoration occurs via the work of the Holy Spirit, who engenders repentance and renews life. The life of the Christian is thus a new one, in which the power and guidance of Christ's Spirit exerts control. The Christian has now entered into the kingdom of God, and the Lord rules via the moral norms of the realm. Christians are now united with Christ, become fellow laborers with him, and are transformed daily into his likeness.

Try a little experiment. Go to Leviticus 19 and read through the laws. See if you can identify which ones are principles, precepts, or rules. Which ones focus on morality, civil society, or holiness? Which ones are formed apodictically, and which are casuistic? I suspect that you will find that many of the laws can be read in more than one way.

For Paul, the salvation that was achieved in Christ is now being fearfully worked out in his followers, and it will one day be fulfilled — when he returns. Morality is the fruit of salvation for the apostle. As a Pharisee, he had previously thought that his moral excellence would earn him salvation. When he met Christ, he realized that this was impossible. Christ is the only one who can keep God's law. Nevertheless, Paul clearly affirms the ongoing role of the law in Christian life when he declares to the Romans:

> The commandments "You shall not commit adultery, You shall not murder, You shall not steal, You shall not covet," and whatever other command there may be, are summed up in this one command: "Love your neighbor as yourself." Love does not harm its neighbor. Therefore love is the fulfillment of the law. (Rom. 13:9-10)

Paul understands that following the rules is not enough for followers of Christ. Or to put it differently, he clearly sees that the demand of love goes beyond that of obedience to law. But this fact does not make the law null and void; in fact, it establishes the law as the foundation for Christian love.

For Jesus, the law has become the rule of the kingdom of God. God rules in the lives of the citizens of his kingdom, and the rules of the kingdom both fulfill and go beyond the laws of the covenant. We hear Jesus enumerate covenant laws in his Sermon on the Mount, but then he gives them a kingdom twist: "You have heard it said, 'Do not kill,' but I tell you that anyone who is angry with a brother or sister will be subject to judgment. . . . Therefore, if you are offering your gift at the altar and remember that your brother or sister has something against you . . . go and be reconciled to that person" (Matt. 5:21-24). Jesus certainly agrees with the covenant law that insists that we do not kill. But merely refraining from murder is not enough for a citizen of God's kingdom. Anger and bitterness are the sources of violence and murder, so in the kingdom it is better to treat the cause of the murder by reconciling with your enemy. This is also true of the laws about adultery, taking oaths, giving alms, and so forth. Jesus showed that, while all of these laws are legitimate, simply observing them is inadequate. In God's kingdom, citizens not only obey the law but seek to transform relationships. The love of God, as seen in his kingdom, demands not only obedience to law but demands initiatives of reconciliation and renewal that transform the whole moral scenery.

Jesus himself is the ideal norm for a Christian's moral life. The life of Jesus as we see it in Scripture, and as it has been embodied in the lives of his followers, serves as a norm for us. This means that the way he was, the things he said, and the deeds he performed are standards for all who profess to follow him. Clearly, we view Jesus from a considerable historical distance, but, even though Jesus is a historical figure, he is at the same time a timeless figure. He was excruciatingly realistic about human weaknesses, forthright in moral judgment about sin, and active in solving the needs of the poor and hurting. His teachings show how we might be kingdom citizens, and his self-sacrifice shows the extent to which love can go. Indeed, what makes Christian ethics Christian might be summed up in this way: being like the Master and doing as the Master does. The fact that Christians follow a person and not an abstract ideal or a code makes it possible to transport his model to a wide range of cultural situations. Jesus is the best human. Other religions cannot claim this about their leaders: all are flawed. But where can you find a better human being than Jesus?

Though it is sometimes assumed that Jesus and Paul said all there was to say about Christian morality, the later New Testament Epistles of Peter, James, and John contribute as well. For Peter, obedience to

The Imitation of Christ

The Imitation of Christ is the title of a book written by Thomas à Kempis, a fifteenth-century Christian who attempted to show how Christ is our norm. This book was a classic of spirituality and moral living in its time and remains a Christian classic today.

God and to civil authorities is paramount. Peter recognizes that sub-ordination to God and the authorities may lead to suffering, but that this is a likely result of following Christ that cannot and should not be avoided. Peter also emphasizes the need for Christians to do what is good and to be holy. The norm for Peter is Christ, and he emphasizes Christ's obedience and willingness to suffer.

The tradition of John (the Gospel, the Letters, and Revelation) clearly establishes love as the norm of Christian life. Love originates with God, who is love (1 John 4:8), and who showed this love for the world (John 3:16). This love focuses first on fellow Christians, for example, "Love one another" (1 John 3:11), "No man has greater love than this, that he lay down his life for his friends" (John 15:13). It then radiates outward (1 John 2:2; 4:14). John turns love into a cycle: God loves us, we love God, God loves the world, and we love each other. The sign that we do love each other is that we keep the commands of the law (John 14:15). And we cannot possibly say that we love God while hating another human being (1 John 3:10; 4:20). The love that we have in Christ obligates us to serve our brothers and neighbors and citizens of the world — not just in word but in deed.

James, the brother of Jesus, uses Jewish wisdom in his Christian ethic. His short letter emphasizes concrete situations of wealth and poverty, faith and works, and so forth. James wants his Jewish Christian readers to consider Jesus as their wise teacher. Jesus the rabbi insists that true faith needs to be shown in deeds of mercy and justice. He sums up his ethic with a revision of Old Testament emphases: "Pure religion, undefiled before God our Father, is this — to visit the father-less and widows in their affliction, and to keep oneself unstained from the world" (James 1:27). James here picks up both sides of the love command: the needy neighbor must be helped, and God must be honored purely.

In summary, we can see that the norm for the Christian life finds its focus in Christ. This focus, however, does not negate the law, but fills it out and shows how important it is for Christians to observe the law.

Ending Questions

1. Explain how Matthew 5:17-20 affirms the continuity of the law as a moral standard even after Jesus "fulfilled the law."
2. List the three roles for God's law as laid out by John Calvin.
3. What does the author mean when he says, "Justice serves as the basis of love, and love fulfills and goes beyond justice"?
4. Describe God's will in terms of the three P's listed by the author.
5. How does the Sabbath law stand as a bridge between the two parts of the Decalogue?
6. Why are Christians no longer required to keep the holiness laws of the Old Testament?
7. Contrast the terms *principle, precept,* and *rules* as they define different levels of law.
8. If human beings are incapable of keeping God's law perfectly, what role does the law play in the lives of the believers?

Works Cited and Further Reading

The difficult topic of Jesus' relationship to the law has received a great deal of scholarly attention recently. You may find the following books helpful in understanding it. Commentaries on the books of Galatians and Romans are also likely to be helpful.

Burridge, Richard. *Imitating Jesus: An Inclusive Approach to New Testament Ethics.* Grand Rapids: Eerdmans, 2007.

Cosgrove, Charles H. *Appealing to Scripture in Moral Debate: Five Hermeneutical Rules.* Grand Rapids: Eerdmans, 2002.

Loader, William. *Jesus' Attitude Towards the Law.* Grand Rapids: Eerdmans, 2002.

Ottati, Douglas. *Jesus Christ and Christian Vision.* Louisville: Westminster John Knox Press, 1996.

Simon, Caroline. *The Disciplined Heart: Love, Destiny, and Imagination.* Grand Rapids: Eerdmans, 1997.

Stassen, Glen H., and David P. Gushee. *Kingdom Ethics: Following Jesus in Contemporary Context.* Downers Grove, IL: InterVarsity Press, 2003.

Verhey, Allen. *Remembering Jesus: Christian Community, Scripture, and the Moral Life.* Grand Rapids: Eerdmans, 2002.

White, R. E. O. *Biblical Ethics.* Atlanta: John Knox Press, 1979.

PART FOUR

Consequences

CHAPTER NINE

Moral Consequences

"I can't hear what you're saying, because what you're doing is drowning you out."

It is important to recognize the potential consequences of our actions. It certainly can be evil not to be concerned about the consequences of what one does. The Nazi Adolf Eichmann was an example of this kind of careless evil. He was a manager who effectively organized the system of deporting Jews from their homes to the death camps. Were his actions wrong? He might answer that they were not: all he did was organize an efficient rail system, just as the manager of any transport business might do. But his organizational skill was used toward a horrific end. When he was captured by the Israeli government in 1960, his claim to be just "following orders" did not save him from the gallows. Because of the evil consequences of his actions, what he did was evil — and he paid the ultimate price for it. (Much of this story is told in the book and movie *The House on Garibaldi Street*.)

Attending to the potential consequences of our actions means that we really do see and do care about what is going on. Developing virtues and following norms is good, but what will be the real results of our actions in the end? This is the question that *consequentialist* ethics asks. The results of what we do are important. As Philip Hallie notes, "Evil doesn't happen only in people's heads." It exists in real deeds. You may have had evil thoughts, but that doesn't make you an evildoer.

For example, you may have once been angry enough to have thoughts about killing someone; perhaps you even came up with a marvelous, police-defying scheme for doing so. But without acting on that thought, you have *done* no evil. Jesus said in the Sermon on the Mount that your murderous thoughts make you guilty of sin. But you are not a murderer.

Accepting the consequences for your actions is also the sign of moral responsibility. Saying "Yes, I am responsible for those outcomes" acknowledges that you are a real actor, not a pawn or a mere re-actor. As I noted in chapter 3 above, a moral agent is a responsible responder.

This chapter will address five questions about moral consequences. First, what kinds of objects are we concerned about? Second, what is the right quantity of consequences? Third, what kinds of good or ill consequences are we talking about? Fourth, what are the criteria for distributing goods and ills? Finally, does the Bible show a preference for some people over others, as far as the distribution of goods is concerned? If so, must we show that preference?

Objects of Moral Concern

If I take a small piece of chalk and crush it under my foot, will you cry for it or get angry with me? I doubt it. You probably don't care much about that little piece of chalk. But what if I were to take your finger and stomp on it with my hard-heeled shoe? I suspect you might then cry out in both pain and anger. There is a real difference between your finger — or anyone else's — and a piece of chalk. That chalk is something you don't care much about; a finger is.

In this illustration, my *action* was the same in both cases: I crushed something with my heel. But the *object* of that action was different: a piece of chalk and your finger. The morality of the deed clearly has to do with the object of the action, not the action itself. Why is this? Why do we evaluate an action taken on one object so differently from the same action taken on another? It is because some things are "objects of moral concern" and others are not. The objects of moral concern are of value to us, so we claim that they have rights and we try to protect them from harm.

You can no doubt sense the difference between the value of one object and another quite readily in the heel-grinding example. You care very little about an inexpensive inanimate object; but you have a strong concern about your finger. After all, you're attached to it! Let's try a couple of more complicated cases to see what kinds of things you value. Most of you probably accept the fact — if you think about it at all — that animals may be killed in order to provide food for humans (though some of you may be principled vegetarians and reject this). But should any animal be eaten? Under what circumstances may it be slaughtered? For example, we get veal by slaughtering young calves that have been kept in pens in the dark (which makes their meat very tender). If you know this and eat veal, you are supporting this treatment of calves. You are making this moral valuation: "My desire for tender meat is of greater value than the life of a calf penned up in the dark." Let's take a more hypothetical — and perhaps improbable — example. Say that a certain species of deer has been declared an endangered species. You have been lost in a vast woods for some time with your family, and you are starving — with no sign of help. In order to survive, you would have to kill the last remaining pair of that deer species. Would you do it? If you do, you are saying that the value of the lives of your family members is greater than the last remaining members of one species of deer.

Humans are creatures who assign value. And the value that we implicitly or explicitly assign to something determines whether it is of moral concern to us. In the above cases, it is likely that you felt a little emotional tug about the poor little calves, or the lone pair of deer of the species. Animals are also objects of moral concern, though generally less so than human lives.

Humans also value plants. For instance, as a gardener I value my bean, lettuce, and tomato plants, and I'll even kill bugs and small rodents that harm them. I desire the good of my plants more than I do the good of those animals. Is this right? Or is there an order of value that must go down from humans, then to animals, and lastly to plants? And does the respect for animals extend to insects such as flies, mosquitoes,

Speciesism

Some animal-rights advocates propose that the value of the life of an animal is equal to that of a human.

They call those of us who value the human species more highly than animals "speciesists." Are you a speciesist? Why or why not?

spiders, and ants? This kind of question not only helps to discover what creatures and/or inanimate things are of moral concern to us, but to discern how much we value each one. Most of us probably value human life most, animal life less, plant life less than animals, and nonliving things least. But as some of the examples above suggest, even among these basic categories of beings, we value some beings more than others.

We also value some beings more at some times than others. For example, you no doubt value your grandmother's life. But when she is very ill and dying, is it of greater value for her to continue to live on for a long time in great pain, or is it better that it be a shorter time with less pain? As another example of this change in valuation, consider the case of an accident in which someone is killed by the negligence of another driver. If you were killed in an accident caused by a reckless or drunk driver when you were in your thirties, had a family, and were working in a well-paid job, the court would award a large sum of money to your survivors. If you were killed at age eighty, without heirs, and never having held a well-paying job, the court would assign your survivors considerably less. These kinds of valuations are being made every day.

Ecological Ethics

Today many ethicists have come to realize that we must value our physical surroundings. In other words, ethics is not just about actions among humans, but it is about actions and virtues that we practice within creation.

We also assign different values to other living things. We value the stately redwood that is hundreds of years old more than we do the pine sapling. We value water more when we are trekking in the desert than when we are vacationing at the lake. We value a polished diamond in the jewelry shop more than an undiscovered gem in a mine.

We all have implicit sets of value, and ethical study helps to clarify them. The Bible does provide some guidance: it places a tremendous value on the lives of human beings. God himself became human, and then gave up that human life because he values it so highly.

How Much?

John Stuart Mill (1806-1873) is the most famous of a group of thinkers known as "utilitarians." In the nineteenth-century England in which

Mill lived, many goods were distributed on the basis of the class or gender of the recipient. For example, if you were a lord, you deserved A, B, C, and D. If you were a commoner, you got only A and B. If you were a woman, you might only get D. Mill saw this as unjust, and he worked within the British Parliament to get laws changed that would produce greater good for all. His principle for action was to do "the greatest good for the greatest number," and his teachings moved England toward a number of social reforms.

Mill sought to promote overall "happiness." By happiness he meant the increase of pleasure and the decrease of pain. He believed that all humans desire happiness, and that his principle thus fit the desire of all humanity. For him, the right action is simply the one that promotes the greatest happiness. Mill recognized that not all pleasures are equal, and thus he placed the intellectual and moral pleasures on a higher plane than the physical ones. He also recognized that the pleasures of all creatures or persons are not equal to one another. In a famous quote from his book *Utilitarianism,* he says: "It is better to be a human being dissatisfied than a pig satisfied; better to be Socrates dissatisfied than a fool satisfied. And if the fool, or the pig, are of a different opinion, it is because they only know their own side of the question." By this Mill demonstrates that the fool and the pig may well be content, but their contentment has far less value than would be the satisfaction of a wise man such as Socrates.

The principle of seeking the greatest good for the greatest number generally works. Think of a few instances. What is the best for all concerned? Isn't greater good better than less? Yes, but things get dicey when we try to put this into practice. How can we be sure that the good outcome we intend will really happen? It is very rare that we can predict the exact outcomes of our actions. There may be a wide range of unintended consequences.

Here's another example of the problem of putting utilitarianism into effect. Let's say that you have ten people and 100 units of some good things, such as fifty-dollar bills, or Thanksgiving turkeys, or concert

Two Variations of Utilitarianism

Act utilitarianism considers the potential pleasure or pain caused by the action we intend. *Rule* utilitarianism says that we must act according to the rule that generally increases pleasure. For example, it is generally better to keep promises; therefore, even if pleasure would be increased in this case by breaking your promise, you should keep it.

tickets. You might automatically assume that the best way to distribute those goods is to give ten to each person. But what if person C needs three times as much of that good and person B hates orchestra concerts? Or, what if three people move away or die? What if the distribution of the goods depends on a certain transportation system, but the system fails? In the table below is another distribution example. The number of goods in Distribution Y is greater than the one in X: twenty-one versus twenty. The number of people involved is the same. Thus simple math would tell us that System Y is the right one, because it provides the greatest good to the same number. Nonetheless, the inequality of Distribution Y is dramatic: persons A, B, and C lose 60 percent of what they had under Distribution X. Which one do you prefer?

	Distribution X	Distribution Y
	Goods	Goods
Person A	5	2
Person B	5	2
Person C	5	2
Person D	5	15

The most difficult objection to the exclusive use of utilitarian ethics is the issue of rights. Might someone have a right to something that overrides the good of the greatest happiness for all? For example, might I have a right to some or all of my property, even if it would serve a greater good to distribute my property and possessions among a large number of poor people?

In an extreme case, consider the following example. There are a limited number of goods in the world, including food, shelter, medical services, and education. Old people in rest homes do not contribute toward the provision of these goods; they only use them up. So, would it not serve the greater good to eliminate the old people in rest homes and then redistribute their goods among a great number of younger producers of goods? A friend of mine who grew up in the Netherlands during World War II witnessed just such a removal of elderly people. When the Nazis invaded the Netherlands, they emptied the rest homes and sent the occupants to their deaths because they were no longer productive citizens.

In a famous story called "The Ones Who Walk Away from Omelas," Ursula LeGuin raises this question of rights versus happiness. She presents the story of a town whose members are as happy as can be imagined. Their health and welfare are fine, their families are caring, their employment is enjoyable, and so on. However, there is a price for this happiness that everyone in Omelas knows. It is that one child of the town must be kept in a dungeon. This child did nothing wrong; he or she is a good child. But in order to maintain the happiness of the group, this child must be kept in the dungeon, in the dark, and alone. When the citizens of Omelas reach adulthood, they are shown the child. Most find the conditions of the child to be repulsive, but they none-theless continue to live in Omelas. A few, however, walk away. Omelas does achieve the greatest good for the greatest number. But would you stay in Omelas knowing that the price to pay for group happiness is violating the rights and the life of one innocent child?

Case Study

Jerry and Lori know that, even though they have no right to a lakefront condo, it would increase their happiness. But what about the welfare of others? The same amount of money they are willing to spend on the condo might pull two dozen families out of desperate poverty. That would ensure the greatest good done for the greatest number of people. Would seeing that good done for so many others actually bring them great happiness?

Kinds of Goods

Is hitting a home run good? How about loving your spouse? How about eating a tasty piece of chocolate cheesecake? I suspect you might say that all of these are good. But which is a greater good? If you say that loving your spouse would be the best good of these three, how much better is it than hitting that home run? We quickly sense that there are different kinds of goods. The home run, the cheesecake, and love for one's spouse are all goods, but they are not of the same kind. Each one has a different end, and the difference in that goal makes the good itself different. A home run, for example, would be of little use in satisfying your needs for love or nutrition, and loving your spouse would not likely boost your runs-batted-in total. This kind of comparison raises the issue of the nature of happiness. Can we say that happiness is one thing that is accomplished in many different ways, or that there are different kinds of happiness?

Utilitarians and many economists who follow them argue that all goods can be lumped together into the one category of "happiness." Then they propose that we can achieve the one condition of happiness in myriad ways. For example, when you buy something for ten dollars, it gives you ten dollars' worth of happy, and something that is worth twenty dollars should normally add twice that amount to your happiness. If the ten-dollar item was a piece of clothing and the twenty-dollar item was a meal, it is obvious that the meal was twice as valuable as the clothing. But if you paid the reverse amounts — twenty for the clothing and ten for the meal — the clothing would be twice as valuable as the meal. Utilitarians do not see this as contradictory. They recognize that at some point different things may produce different amounts of happiness.

I do not believe that all of our goals can be reduced to the one measure of happiness. The kind of satisfaction I receive from hitting a home run is qualitatively different from the love of my spouse or the taste of the cheesecake. This has implications for what we do. If we seek only the one goal of happiness, then everything we do is nothing but an instrument used in the pursuit of that happiness. If, however, there are really different goals that can't be measured on the same scale, then we may act out of a wide range of motivations, in a wide range of ways, in pursuit of a wide range of ends.

This argument uses a basic distinction among goods: *instrumental* goods and *intrinsic* goods. Intrinsic goods are things that are thought to be good in themselves, whereas instrumental goods are good for something. For example, is it good to feed someone who is starving? You will no doubt say yes, and if I were to ask you to explain why it is good, you might be puzzled. You might simply respond that, if another human is suffering from starvation and you can relieve that suffering, you should. This seems to be a good in itself, and it defies the need for explanation. When you get to this point, where no further explanation is necessary, you have arrived at an intrinsic good: it is simply good.

But how will you help those who are starving? Will you send a check to OXFAM, or to your church? Will you go to the place where they live and give them some food? Will you lobby the government on their behalf? The way that you go about doing this good is an instrumental good. There are many possible instruments you could use to achieve the intrinsic good you seek. It might be best to write the check, or go to their house, or lobby the government in different situations. In each case you will be aiming at your intrinsic good by means of various instruments.

Saint Augustine believed that the basic moral problem with human beings is that we see something as an intrinsic value when it really has only instrumental value. For example, we might seek wealth. But wealth is only an instrument that allows us to do other things. For Augustine, the ultimate value is God. All other things or ideas must be used in the service of knowing and serving God. God himself is the only thing/person that we cannot use for something else, since God himself is the ultimate good.

Criteria for Distribution of Goods

The next issue is this: How do we decide how to distribute goods and ills? Or what are the criteria we use for distribution? Let me provide a concrete example. Let's say that you are the parent of two children whose ages are five and fifteen years old. When it is time for dinner, you give the fifteen-year-old three times more food than you give the five-year-old, and each child eats the amount given. But when it comes to dessert, you give the five-year-old an equal share to that of the fifteen-year-old. Are you being fair in either case: to give the fifteen-year-old three times more of the dinner, or the five-year-old an equal share of dessert?

In situations like these we have set criteria for distribution that enable us to quantify the amount distributed. In this case, we seem to assume that each child has his size-related need for nutritional calories, and that satisfying this need is accomplished by giving the older child three times more dinner than the younger. But dessert seems more like a treat or favor than a satisfier of hunger. So we distribute dessert on the grounds of equality. To give one child more dessert might suggest that you love one more than another; to give one child less food than they need for nutrition seems unjust. Most of us make these kinds of judgments daily, in an automatic and unreflective way. In the case of this family, need and equality are the two criteria that determined how much each child receives.

In other situations, there may be other standards that guide our distribution of goods, such as skill or aptitude or proximity. In each case, a different criterion is used, yielding a just distribution. The most skilled athlete will start on the basketball team; the student with the most scholarly potential will be given the academic scholarship; and the child who is my offspring will get the food.

Therefore, a crucial question in addressing distribution of goods or ills is: What is your criterion for distribution? The political philosopher Michael Walzer suggests that goods should be distributed in light of the sphere of life they are part of. For example, in a family or similar group, most goods should be distributed on the basis of the *need* of its members. In a business or marketplace, most goods should be distributed on the basis of the *contribution* that each person has made to the productivity of the firm. In a nation, most goods — such as access to roads, services, or the court system — should be distributed on the basis of *equality*.

I tend to agree with Walzer. But consider this conclusion that I might draw from his ideas. As a Christian, I believe that all humans are part of the one family of God's children. In a family, things should be distributed on the basis of each family member's need. Should I, therefore, sacrifice goods that I have until the needs of all or many other members are met?

An important and related question is this: Who chooses the criterion for distribution? The practical answer is that a great range of people choose in a wide range of contexts. In the family the parent or guardian chooses. In the marketplace the businesspeople choose what to produce and how much to charge, while consumers choose how much they are willing to pay. The government

Distributive Justice

The issue we address here is called "distributive justice," and it is a pretty straightforward and clear title for the issue.

The ancient Roman jurist Ulpian said: "Justice is the constant and perpetual desire to render to each his due."

But questions such as those we have been asking quickly arise:

Who decides?

What is the criterion for distribution?

Does "each" mean each member of my family, or state, or world?

How do we see to it that each actually gets his or her due?

makes decisions about how many things should be distributed. In socialist societies, for example, the government or party in power makes nearly all the decisions about how many things are distributed. In a remote village, on the other hand, local farmers might decide about the distribution of most goods. This issue is the realm of political justice that is fought over and debated on a daily basis. A current example being debated in the United States is health care. Who deserves to receive health-care benefits — everyone with a job? all citizens? all people living in the United States? And so forth.

Advocacy

Most people assume a high value for their own lives and that of other humans. However, we may implicitly value those who are of our nation or race or family more highly than those who are different from us. This is the point at which theologians remind us that all humans are created equally as God's children. It is not only men, or white people, people with wealth, or left-handed people who are related to God as his own children, but people of color, women, the poor, and so on. In the past the objects of our moral concern were often members of our family, tribe, or nation. Christian faith calls us beyond those boundaries. As Jesus says, "As you have done to the least of these, you have done it to me."

One way of looking at the validity of an ethical system, then, is to see who it serves. Who are the objects of its moral concern? If the answer is that the system serves its designers well, we should be suspicious. If it serves a particular class or race or kind of people better than others, it is likely to be unjust. The question that must be asked is: Whom does this outcome favor?

Liberation theologians, feminists, and others argue that the most important criterion in determining just outcomes is to identify the kind of people who will be aided and those who will be harmed. They maintain that the people who need the most help are the very ones who have been harmed by political-economic systems in the past. In recent years, women have justifiably demanded that economic outcomes not favor men. People of color have made the same reasonable demand. It is clear that outcomes have been weighted in favor of some groups in the past. The tough question that then arises is whether there should be compensatory favor shown to the groups who have suffered discrimination in the past. What do you think?

When liberation theologians say that God has a "preferential option" for the poor, they mean that God takes the side of the poor, the outcast, and the marginalized, and stands up for them. Jesus did this. When he preached his first sermon, he quoted from Isaiah and applied the words to himself:

> The Spirit of the Lord is upon me
> > because he has anointed me to bring good news to the poor.
> He has sent me to proclaim release to the captives,
> > and recovery of sight to the blind,
> > to let the oppressed go free,
> to proclaim the year of the Lord's favor. (Luke 4:18)

There are more than a hundred other references to poverty and the poor in Scripture. Among them are the following, which support the position of liberation theology.

> "There will never be any poor among you if only you obey the LORD your God by carefully keeping these commandments which I lay upon you this day. . . ." (Deut. 15:4)

> "Take heart, you seekers after God, for the LORD listens to the poor and does not despise his captive people." (Ps. 69:32-33)

> "He who is generous to the poor lends to the LORD, who will recompense him for his deed." (Prov. 19:17)

> "Woe to those who enact unjust laws and draft oppressive edicts, depriving the poor of justice, robbing the weakest of my people of their rights, plundering the widow and despoiling the fatherless." (Isa. 10:1-2)

"Has not God chosen those who are poor in the eyes of the world to be rich in faith and to possess the kingdom he promised to those who love him?" (James 2:5)

In these and numerous other texts, God shows a deep concern for the poor and the marginalized. The poor, in turn, have no one to turn to but God. This special relationship of absolute dependence places the poor in an exalted place within the kingdom of God. They are the ones whom the kingdom brings out of misery into joy, and they are the ones that Christians are called to lift up. So if the consequences of our actions do not benefit the poor and the marginalized, we are not doing good for those for whom God cares the most.

Summarizing Consequentialism

Consequences are important. Saying that we are virtuous or principled is not enough. We must act, and we must take responsibility for what we do. The things or persons that we concern ourselves with are important indicators of our ethics. If we are unconcerned about others or about the creation, we are missing part of the gospel message. Doing the greatest good for the greatest number is a handy rule of thumb, but it is difficult to put into practice. We must determine who or what is the object of our moral concern. We must determine what criterion we will use to distribute the good or ill. The criteria may change from one sphere of life to another, or even from one time to another. We must keep in mind that it is God's preference to do good for those who are the weakest and poorest in society.

Liberation Theology

This movement began in 1968, when the Catholic bishops of Latin American met in Medellín, Colombia. There they insisted that the Bible mandates "a preferential option for the poor."

This theology emphasizes that we must act in favor of the poor, and then reflect on what we have done. They call this process "praxis" (a cycle of reflection-action-reflection).

This way of doing theology is contrasted with traditional European theology, which has assumed that theology begins with ideas and doctrines that may (or may not) be put into practice.

Ending Questions

1. Being concerned with consequences is often contrasted with being concerned with norms. Someone concerned with norms would say, "Just do the right thing — no matter what the consequences." The consequentialist says, "Figure out what will bring about the greatest good — no matter what the norm demands." Which is right? Can both be?

2. If I make no attempt to find out what the consequences of my actions will be, am I committing a moral wrong?

3. If we would attempt to calculate the consequences of each of our actions, we would likely be paralyzed by inaction. What is the solution to this?

4. Is it right to be more concerned about some people than about others?

5. Rank the things/beings that you are concerned with from greatest to least.

Works Cited and Further Reading

Bouma-Prediger, Steven. *For the Beauty of the Earth.* 2nd ed. Grand Rapids: Baker Books, 2010.

Hallie, Philip. "The Evil That Men Think — and Do." *Hastings Center Report,* December 1985.

LeGuin, Ursula. "The Ones Who Walk Away from Omelas." In *The Wind's Twelve Quarters: Stories.* New York: Harper & Row, 1975.

Mill, John Stuart. *Utilitarianism.* Dover, UK: Thrift Editions, 2004.

Rasmussen, Larry. *Earth Community, Earth Ethics.* Maryknoll, NY: Orbis, 1996.

Sittler, Joseph. *Evocations of Grace: Writings on Ecology, Theology, and Ethics.* Grand Rapids: Eerdmans, 2000.

Van Til, Kent. *Less than $2.00 a Day: A Christian View of World Poverty and the Free Market.* Grand Rapids: Eerdmans, 2007.

Walzer, Michael. *Spheres of Justice: A Defense of Pluralism and Equality.* New York: Basic Books, 1983.

Zimmerman, Michael J. "Intrinsic vs. Extrinsic Value." In *The Stanford Encyclopedia of Philosophy,* edited by Edward N. Zalta (Fall 2008 edition).

CHAPTER TEN

Ultimate Ends

"WHAT DO YOU want to be when you grow up?" Perhaps you were asked that question as a child, or you will ask it of your children or grandchildren. Depending on the stage of life you are in, the question can be quite important. If you are in college, the answer to this question will likely determine which course of study you pursue, or perhaps it already has determined which college you decided to attend. The reason is obvious: in order to get somewhere, you have to aim in the right direction. Unless you are going somewhere in particular, you will accomplish little by setting off.

So where are we going? As Christians our ultimate answer will be something like this: to live at peace and in joy with God in the new creation. That will be the place where we are accepted by God and will live in glorious splendor as friends of God. This fantastic picture of the future for all Christians is our hope.

The next question — how will you get there? — is the question of the Christian life. If our goal is a life of delight with God in the age to come, we must aim toward such a life in this age. In this final chapter I will work from that future back into the present. In other words, I will describe the end of life as depicted in Scripture and then will trace back a path that will lead to it. The Bible gives us a range of images and ideas that describe our ultimate destiny. I will take some of these images of the future, and then pull their significance back into the moral life of the Christian at present. The images and ideas I'll address are:

- Our ultimate concern
- The kingdom of God
- Our vocation and deeds
- The final judgment
- The connection of our deeds from this world to the next
- The renewal of our bodies and of the world

Our Ultimate Concern

Theologian Paul Tillich has said that religion is our "ultimate concern." By this he means that the thing, or person, or idea that most concerns us and compels us to action is, at bottom, our religion. Perhaps another way of saying that is that the thing we love most is a god to us. So, what *is* our ultimate object of concern? It could be our faith, our family, our nation, our profession and earning power, our dreams of success, or what have you. Knowing what the object of our ultimate concern is, is most important because the thing that we aim at determines where we go. If we aim at a happy family life, our actions and virtues will shape themselves to that end. If we seek financial success, our virtues and actions will serve that goal.

Ethics has long raised the issue of our ultimate end(s). The Greeks asked, "What is the good life?" They philosophized about the end — or goal — of life that would be best for humans, their *summum bonum,* or greatest good. They then proposed ways of life that would lead to that good. Socrates said that an unexamined life would not be worth living. In this chapter we will examine the greatest good of life as it is found in the Christian faith.

The Christian disciple, by definition, is one whose greatest good is found in Christ. That ultimate concern should shape every aspect of our current life. It demands much of us and requires absolute dedication. The fact that it is an ultimate goal may yield the result of martyrdom, since Christianity and other ultimate value systems admit that this life is worth less than our ultimate good.

Any good thing outside of God is insufficient to bear the weight of the most profound human aspirations. Any ultimate goal that is not

God disappoints, and seeking or even finding it is futile. Goals such as self-indulgence or happiness seem to be the ultimate desire of many, but they are not sufficient to fill our ultimate aspiration. Self-fulfillment is an end that does not lead us beyond ourselves; it may only indulge a person who is set on pleasing herself. Without God as the ultimate good, we attach ourselves to lesser goods or gods, whether they be ourselves, our group, our political agenda, or our notions of success and happiness. It is difficult to surpass Augustine's analysis of this issue.

The Westminster Shorter Catechism

The very first question of the Westminster Catechism addresses this important question of ultimate goals:

Q: What is the chief end of man?

A: To glorify God, and to enjoy him forever.

> How then, according to reason, ought man to live? We all certainly desire to live happily; and there is no human being but assents to this statement almost before it is made. But the title happy cannot, in my opinion, belong either to him who has not what he loves, whatever it may be, or to him who has what he loves, if it is hurtful, or to him who does not love what he has, although it is good in perfection. For one who seeks what he cannot obtain suffers torture, and one who has got what is not desirable is cheated, and one who does not seek for what is worth seeking for is diseased. . . . I find, then, a fourth case, where the happy life exists, — when that which is man's chief good is both loved and possessed. For what do we call enjoyment but having at hand the object of love?

According to Augustine, not being able to get your goal is torture, getting something that is not worthy cheats you, and going after something that is not worthy is a disease. The only way to have a happy life is to seek and find the ultimate worthy end, and that end is God. All humans are seekers. We know that this life is not all that it can be. The longing for a future life with God is at the heart of the Christian hope. Hebrews 11:13-16 says:

> All these died in faith. Although they had not received the things promised, yet they had seen them far ahead and welcomed them, and acknowledged themselves to be strangers and aliens without

fixed abode on earth. Those who speak in that way plainly show that they are looking for a country of their own. If their thoughts had been with the country they had left, they could have found opportunity to return. Instead, we find them longing for a better country, a heavenly one. That is why God is not ashamed to be called their God; for he has a city ready for them.

The Kingdom of God

Jesus is clear about our ultimate goal. He said, "Seek first the kingdom of God, and its righteousness, and all these things will be added to you." The "all these things" that will be added were the basic needs of everyday life that he had just been talking about (Matt. 6:25-34). The kingdom that Jesus told us to seek is exactly what Jesus himself taught about and demonstrated. For example, his healings showed that life in the kingdom is one in which people are physically whole and sane. His feedings showed that those in the kingdom do not suffer from hunger or want. His teachings on the kingdom tell us that the first will be last, and the last first. Yet Jesus also preached and taught that the kingdom is yet to come, and that we should seek it, as it is still to be realized in its entirety. We now recognize that the kingdom of God will not be brought to fruition until the Second Coming of Christ. In that kingdom, God's will shall be done on earth just as it is in heaven. Then there will be perfect justice, peace, and the complete restoration of the poor, the weak, and the despised.

Central to the reign of God is justice. As the text says, "Seek the kingdom *and its righteousness.*" The translation of the word "righteousness" might be updated in our time with the word "justice." It is the justice of the kingdom that is to be so fervently sought. Seeking justice is accomplished not simply by prayer, though prayer is crucial. Seeking justice entails constantly *doing* justice. Much of Jesus' own ministry was aimed at bringing about justice. For example, he challenged the view of the law as interpreted by the Pharisees, in which the Sabbath was observed by following small formal rules rather than by doing works of mercy. Jesus challenged those who were about to stone an adulterous woman to death, showing that the righteousness/justice of those setting out to stone her was no greater than hers.

The Old Testament prophets, like Jesus after them, warn that we cannot claim to seek God if we do not do his justice. For example, Isaiah writes:

> Your countless sacrifices, what are they to me? says the Lord.
>> I am sated with whole-offerings of rams and the fat of
>>> well-fed cattle;
>> I have no desire for the blood of bulls, of sheep, and of he-goats,
>> when you come into my presence.
>> Who has asked you for all this?
>> No more shall you tread my courts.
>> To bring me offerings is futile;
>> The reek of sacrifice is abhorrent to me. . . .
>> Wash and be clean;
>> Put away your evil deeds far from my sight;
>> Cease to do evil, learn to do good.
>> Pursue justice, guide the oppressed;
>> Uphold the rights of the fatherless, and plead the widow's cause.
>
> (Isa. 1:11-16)

How is the life of the Christian shaped by the coming kingdom? It is seen in the ways in which we seek God and promote God's justice. Creating kingdom-like justice in the present is the task of the kingdom disciple.

Our Vocation and Deeds

The thesis of this chapter is that the goal we pursue shapes who we are now. For example, if I seek excellence as a piano player, I am on my way to becoming a pianist. Practicing the piano does not just add agility to my fingers; it enables me to pursue the vocation of a pianist. What is true of performing on a musical instrument is also true of practicing a trade, playing a sport, doing experiments in a laboratory, or studying in the library. It aids us in becoming persons who can realize a vocation.

Our practices shape the kind of person we are becoming, not only in terms of our career but also in terms of our character. The life we live now is a preparation for a future life, and our present moral practice shapes the future that we will enjoy.

God calls all Christians to be followers of Christ, but each one of us discerns a particular vocation in which we fill out this calling. Completion of a divinely given vocation can be a great joy, be it parenting, serving school lunches, or running a corporation. All of us are called to serve God, and the mandate to "cultivate and care for the earth" is the task of all. If my vocation is to serve school lunches in the cafeteria, then fulfilling that calling is as proper and important for me as it would be to be the pastor of America's largest church. All vocations (unless explicitly immoral) can be part of the Christian's calling. Discovering one's vocation can be difficult, though most people in the developed nations of the world have many opportunities to do so. On the other hand, the poor in this country and many other countries don't have the opportunity to develop their skills, change careers, or pursue advanced education as we do. Their humanity is thus diminished since they cannot live out their divinely given potential. A crucial task for Christians with resources, then, is to increase the opportunities for those who have very few of them.

Caroline Simon reminds us of the importance of the imagination in this process of finding and fulfilling our vocation. We first imagine who the person is that we wish to become. When we imagine, we don't have God's perfect vision, but we do have his perfect grace. Imagining rightly, then, is seeing who we as the best kingdom citizens can become with the eyes of grace. Our lives become a process of working out the selves that we can, with God's grace, become.

Fiction-making, in contrast with graced imagining, is creating a

The Elixir
George Herbert

Teach me, God and King,
In all things thee to see,
And what I do in anything,
To do it as for thee.

A servant with this clause
Makes drudgery divine,
Who sweeps a room, as for thy law,
Makes that and th' action fine.

This is the famous stone
That turneth all to gold:
For that which God doth touch and own
Cannot for less be told.

false self, one who is not in tune with God's music. Fiction-making pretends that the person we are becoming need not be in harmony with the life of holiness, love, and justice to which God calls us. Fiction-making pushes others into the molds that we create for them rather than encouraging them to live out life within the frame of experience and joy that God has for them. Fiction-making is egoistic; it is wishful thinking. If only I were . . . If only he were . . . If only she . . . If only they . . . In short, fiction-making is self-deception and self-delusion. It is telling ourselves that we are who we are not, and telling others that they are humans who they are not.

The advertising genius Leo Burnett challenged his employees with these words:

"Reach for the stars. You may not grasp them, but you won't come up with a handful of dirt."

Role models are important in getting our imagination right. Whom would you want to be like? The gorgeous and sexy movie star, the wildly successful businessman, or the powerful political leader? It's unlikely, but it is possible for you to become one of these. But if you practice at becoming one of these instead of your true vocation, you would be destroying the true self to which God calls you.

Discerning your true self is done in community. We can help each other by honestly noting each other's gifts and weaknesses. When infants are baptized in my church, the pastor asks the congregation: "Do you, the people of the Lord, promise to receive these children in love, pray for them, instruct them in the faith, and encourage and sustain them in the fellowship of believers?" We answer yes, and thus we take communal responsibility for the future of this child of God. Believers who know Christ promise to encourage and sustain new believers and children, as they seek to live into the vision of Christ to which they are called.

The self we become is also largely determined by the commitments we make. To be without commitments makes us less human. Taking on too many commitments requires that we become superhuman. Commitments create our future, and our greatest commitment creates the greatest future. Christian life begins and ends with a commitment to follow Christ, and the pursuit of Christ can include suffering for him. It also includes a shaping into his form and character. Someone who is committed to Christ is necessarily part of the family of Christ, or the church. Our commitment to the church identifies not only where we are going but with whom we go.

The fact that there is a divine destiny for all of us plays out in the course of a lifetime. This destiny is to see God, and to become as he is. No one can fulfill all of his/her aspirations or use all of his/her capabilities in one lifetime. There are opportunity costs. Pursuing a degree in theology meant I had less time to practice the piano. Marrying my wife meant that I could not marry any other woman. Living in Wisconsin meant I could not live in San Jose, Costa Rica, at the same time. Fulfillment cannot mean that we do all that we could do. Human limitation prevents this. But God gives us a present life to live and a future life that holds endless possibilities.

The Final Judgment

It is necessary that sin and evil be judged and then eliminated upon the consummation of the kingdom of God. God is absolutely good and true, and sin is absolutely evil and false. The fullness of God's presence in his kingdom entails the elimination of sin and evil. It is not possible that impurity and contamination could exist in the presence of a perfectly holy God. It would be as if dry leaves could survive in a blast furnace.

God's demand for justice entails the necessity of a final judgment. When you or I are wronged, we seek justice. We want compensation. We want to see that each person gets what he or she deserves. Inasmuch as we want justice when we are wronged, God, too, seeks justice. Justice is ultimately God's, and judgment is his as well. Yet God's justice triumphs as his love overcomes. God does not judge us on the basis of what we do; he judges on the basis of what Christ has done for us. Therefore, those who approach God on the basis of Christ's justice are saved.

There are various judgments of peoples and individuals throughout history, but there is one judgment that occurs at the end of history. That judgment shows that all of history has been in the hands of God. The provisional judgments on individuals and peoples throughout history are precursors of a final judgment for all. At the center of historical judgment was the incarnation of Christ; the end of history will be the Second Coming of Christ, leading to the Last Judgment. All of history is guided by and brought to fruition by God, and the standard of judgment throughout history is the relationship each has to the Son of righteousness. Christ stands at the center and at the end of history, and it is he who shall "judge the living and the dead."

Case Study

John must admit that watching pornography is fiction-making. Are he and his genitals really magnets for beautiful women? Are women's bodies really all around him only so that he can gain sexual pleasure from them? What he is imagining is not his true self, nor theirs.

At the Last Judgment each life will be shown for what it is. The general resurrection restores the unity of body and soul that was lost at death, and it sets all before the judgment seat of God. Then all is revealed, and true justice is rendered. Our thoughts and words, as well as our deeds, come under God's judgment (Matt. 12:36; Rom. 2:16). The fact that the thoughts, words, and deeds of this lifetime have consequences for life everlasting in the kingdom of God vindicates and strengthens the moral order that God has created in this world. In other words, our thoughts, words, and deeds in this life have everlasting consequences.

Knowledge is again a factor in the degree of responsibility we have when we are judged, as it was when we assumed responsibility as moral agents. That is, in the end times, those who knew little about God and his morality will be less responsible for their deeds than those who knew much. For example, in Matthew 10:15 Jesus tells the disciples whom he has sent to preach in the towns of Israel that "on the Day of Judgment it will be more bearable for the land of Sodom and Gomorrah than for that town" (one in Israel that rejected his message). There are also indications that those who have not heard the gospel at all will be held to a lower standard than those who knew it (Rom. 2:12). The point is clear: while all are responsible to varying degrees, all must respond to God in Christ.

Saint Paul speaks about his anticipation of the life to come: "It is not that I have already achieved this. I have not yet reached perfection, but I press on, hoping to take hold of that for which Christ once took hold of me. My friends, I do not claim to have hold of it yet. What I do say is this: forgetting what is behind and straining towards what lies ahead, I press on towards the finishing line, to win the heavenly prize to which God has called me in Christ Jesus" (Phil. 3:12-14). Notice how active Paul is here. There is not only an aspect of waiting and hoping for the future, but of being eager to grasp it and be worthy of it. Perfection is his goal, and he can see the goal ahead in Jesus Christ.

The Connection of Deeds from This Life to the Next

There appear to be two ways in which the words and deeds of this life affect the life to come. First, our deeds show whether we truly have been saved. Secondly, our deeds determine the nature and extent of our reward.

In the judgment story that Jesus tells in Matthew 25:31-46, the Son of man first separates the nations into sheep and goats, and then gives the reason for the separation — their deeds. Those who are given the inheritance of God showed that they knew him by meeting strangers and taking them in, by visiting prisoners, and by clothing the naked. On the other hand, those who by their inaction showed that they did not know God are cursed and sent to the eternal fire. The connection between the deeds we do and the reward we receive is all too clear. We cannot say that we are one of Christ's faithful flock if we do not show love to others who suffer. The proof of who we are is in our deeds.

James, the brother of Jesus, provides the same lesson in other terms:

> What good is it, my friends, for someone to say he has faith when his actions do nothing to show it? Can that faith save him? . . . But someone may say: "One chooses faith, another action." To which I reply: "Show me this faith you speak of with no actions to prove it, while I by my actions will prove to you my faith. . . ." As the body is dead when there is no breath in it, so faith divorced from action is dead. (James 2:14, 18, 26)

In Revelation 20 we witness a scene of the judgment. "The Book of the Deeds of Men" is opened, and it appears to be a moral registry. It is simply recorded that "the dead were judged from the things that were written in the book, according to their works." It is clear from these and other passages that works are evidence of faith.

It is less clear, but nevertheless certain, that deeds done in this life also shape the nature and extent of our reward in the next. Four passages in particular are instructive: Luke 19:12-27, 1 Corinthians 3:5-15, Revelation 20, and Revelation 22:12-13. The Luke passage tells of a ruler who takes a journey and gives his servants a sum of money to use in his absence. Upon his return, the ruler demands a reckoning. The servants who have gained a return on their investments are rewarded in proportion to their gain: a tenfold gain merits rule over ten cities, a fivefold gain over five. One servant, however, does nothing with the money his master has entrusted to him. The ruler not only gives this servant no cities, but he takes away the initial sum of money he has given him.

In 1 Corinthians 3:5-15, Paul speaks of the work of building the church. He notes that each builder contributes in different ways and at different points. But the work of each will be tested on the final day. On that day, a fire of purification will test the material that each has used: straw, hay, precious stones, or wood. "The fire will test the worth of each person's work. If anyone's building survives, he will be rewarded; if it burns down, he will have to bear the loss; yet he will escape with his life, though only by passing through the fire" (1 Cor. 3:13-15). It seems that salvation for the builder is secure, but the works of each builder are of different value. Some are of inestimable value, and others of little if any. Those who build with valuable material are rewarded in kind.

The remaining passages are brief. Jesus says, "For the Son of man is to come in the glory of his Father with his angels, and then he will give everyone his due reward" (Matt. 16:27). In Revelation 22:12-13, God says: "I am coming soon, and bringing with me my recompense to repay everyone according to what he has done! I am the Alpha and the Omega, the first and the last, the beginning and the end." Though clear, these statements leave much unspecified. Jesus is bringing a reward, but we are not told the exact nature of that compensation. The basis for compensation is what each one has done, but the passage does not specify the exact nature of the deeds either. That day will be a summing up of all that we have been, and all that we have become.

As I have mentioned above, the fact that reward is based on the works of this lifetime is clear. The kind of reward and the nature of the deeds is not as clear. In broad terms, many good works garner a great and good reward. Other passages also indicate that there is to be a great diversity in levels of glory in the world to come (Matt. 10:15; 11:24; 23:14; 24:51; 16:27; 19:29; 25:15-23; Luke 6:38; 10:12-14; 12:46-47; 19:13-19; Rom. 2:6; 1 Cor. 3:8; 2 Cor. 4:17; 5:10; 9:6; Gal. 6:8-9; Heb. 11: 26; Rev. 2:23; 11:18; 20:12; 22:12). These passages indicate that, while all believers are saved, there are degrees and kinds of glory. For example, Abraham is depicted by Jesus as sitting at the right hand of God; twelve are seen as seated around God's throne; many are set as judges of the angels. God confers eternal life on all who believe, but God glorifies each person according to what he or she has done.

Bodily Renewal and the Renewal of the World

The new creation is neither the continuation of the world just as it has been nor its destruction, but a renewal and cleansing of this world (Matt. 5:18; 24:35; 2 Pet. 3:10; Heb. 1:11-12; 1 John 2:17; Rev. 21:1). There are five reasons for believing that this world is not to be destroyed, but renewed. First, God redeems and renews *this* humanity, and *this* world. Were he to destroy this world and start over, it would imply that Satan had won. Second, the Greek term used for making things "new" in 2 Peter 3:13 and Revelation 21:1 is *kainos,* not *neos. Kainos* implies newness in kind or quality, rather than new in time or origin, as the term *neos* would imply. Third, many of the terms in passages of judgment are images of purification. Throughout the biblical story, fire and water are used as purifying agents (Num. 19:12; Ezek. 36:25; Isa. 30:27-33; Mal. 3:2; Mark 9:49; 1 Cor. 3:13; Eph. 5:26; Heb. 10:22; 12:29; 1 Pet. 3:21; 2 Pet. 3:3-7). Fourth, in Romans 8:19-21, Paul says that the creation moans for its liberation from evil and decay. He does not say it yearns for annihilation or a complete start-over. Finally, as the bodies of believers are contiguous with the resurrected body, we expect that the future earth will be contiguous with the present earth as well.

This view of the future of this world is significant for the present. It shows us that the present world is not something evil that should be escaped or disparaged, but that it is a corrupted good that needs purification. It implies an ecological ethic in which the physical world is valued as a good in its own right. It also reminds us of the cosmic extent of God's redemption. The salvation of God does not mean that souls are to be spared from the flames, but that the entire world should be renewed and will then experience the joy of life with God. For this reason it is wrong to look on the created world or on its creatures or persons only as instruments that help us find satisfaction. They are valuable in their own right.

In the world to come, God lives with his people. The cultures of this world will spill over into the New Jerusalem. "Nations will journey to the light of the New Jerusalem, and kings to its radiance. . . . Seaborne riches will be lavished on her, and the wealth of nations will be hers" (Isa. 60:3, 5b). "Foreigners will rebuild your walls and their kings will be your servants. . . . Your gates will stand open at all times; day and night they will never be shut, so that through them may be brought the wealth of nations and their kings under escort" (Isa. 60:10a, 11). The picture here in Isaiah, as well as the one in Revelation, is one of a fantastic new city, not a new garden of Eden. The collected goods of human culture are present. There will be both material and spiritual blessings in the city of God. Tribes and nations will contribute to this new world (Rev. 5:9; 7:9; 21:24-26). All the various languages and peoples are present. The wealth of the world is present. It is the world that humans have cultivated and guarded that is renewed in the age to come. The vision of John in Revelation attempts to portray the glory of the future. John sees that the blessed are free from sin and its effects. We carry out God's will in this world, and we find our future in the world that is renewed by a triumphant Christ. We enjoy life with God in a perfected world.

It also seems appropriate that the kind of reward that each of us receives will be uniquely suited to the kind of person we have become. For example, I would consider it no reward whatsoever to listen to country music for eternity. It is at least conceivable, however, that some fans of that music might. Friends of mine who enjoy designing and building things would likely see heaven as a place to construct things and remodel at will, free from the frustrations of paperwork, codes, and permits. Though Scripture is not explicit on this point, it seems that inasmuch as we are particular people with particular gifts, our unique characteristics will shape our unique reward. From the parables of the talents, it appears that what we do in this life gives us a capacity for what we will do in the life to come. For example, if all I did in this lifetime were to drink beer and watch sports, I would have very little capacity to do much in the life to come. However, if I fully develop the gifts that God has given me in this lifetime, I will be able to use them in the life to come.

The eternal life is an everlasting Sabbath in which we enjoy the world as it was created to be, and live within it as Christ has freed us to live. However, this does not imply idleness. We will continue to serve God and to rule as kings; we will be given great authority, in proportion to that which we have done on earth (Matt. 24:47; 25:21-23); we will be called on to judge angels, and so forth. The activities of the new heaven and earth will no longer be characterized by toil and frustration, but by discovery and delight. The contrast between this world of misery and heavenly joy will be removed: God will "wipe away every tear from our eyes." The fact that we will be in Christ, and that Christ will be all in all, removes the possibility that any future sin will undo the present redemption. We shall be no longer able to sin, because we will be in Christ, the sinless one.

The restoration of humanity is a moral one, not just a physical one. We will not be made into different humans, but into proper humans. The fact that we have a human body is not the problem; it is the alienation between each human person and God. To put it another way, the resurrection does not mean that we will receive new spirits, or become new creatures; rather, we become the glorious and glorified humans we always were meant to be. The fact that we have a body that will be recognizably our own suggests that our person, with our gifts, will be the very one who continues to exist in eternity. (The fact that Jesus had his own body after his resurrection indicates that we will as well.) The fact that we are granted a renewed body reinforces the significance of the things we now do in the body.

Allow me to summarize. We will reign with Christ in the new creation. We will live in joy and peace in the presence of God. We will be purified by the Spirit. We will receive our inheritance and reward. Therefore, we should become the persons who are worthy to reign with Christ. We should become the persons who can stand before God in peace. We should do works that store up treasure and reward in heaven. And we should live into the vocation to which God has called us.

Ending Questions

1. St. Augustine famously said, "O Lord, you have made us for yourself, and our souls are restless till they rest in you." Does this mean that Christians have necessarily achieved happiness — or found their ultimate end?
2. Do you agree that God has a "preferential option for the poor"?
3. What practical steps can you take to promote God's justice?
4. Because of life circumstances and human frailties, few people actually become the ideal self that they imagine. Should those who do not become such ideal persons feel guilty?
5. What if the world did not end with a Judgment?
6. How do you imagine heaven? What capacities are you now building in yourself to enjoy it?
7. Theologians strain to understand how the Book of the Deeds and the Book of Life as found in Revelation relate to each other. What do you think?
8. Our culture idolizes some kinds of selves. Which, if any of these, are agreeable to the self that Christ calls you to?

Works Cited and Further Reading

Alcorn, Randy. *Heaven.* Carol Stream, IL: Tyndale, 2004.

Aurelius Augustine. "On the Morals of the Catholic Church." In *The Works of Aurelius Augustine,* edited by M. Dods. Edinburgh: T. & T. Clark, 1892.

Bavinck, Herman. *The Last Things.* Translated by John Vriend. Grand Rapids: Baker Books, 1996.

Hill, Craig. *In God's Time: The Bible and the Future.* Grand Rapids: Eerdmans, 2002.

Hoekema, Anthony. *The Bible and the Future.* Grand Rapids: Eerdmans, 1979.

Mouw, Richard. *When the Kings Come Marching In: Isaiah and the New Jerusalem.* Grand Rapids: Eerdmans, 1983.

Schuurman, Douglas. *Vocation: Discerning our Callings in Life.* Grand Rapids: Eerdmans, 2003.

Simon, Caroline. *The Disciplined Heart: Love, Destiny, and Imagination.* Grand Rapids: Eerdmans, 1997.

Wall, Robert W. *Revelation.* Peabody, MA: Hendrickson, 1991.

Index